College Writing

2

HOUGHTON MIFFLIN
ENGLISH FOR ACADEMIC SUCCESS

Eileen Cotter
Montgomery College

SERIES EDITORS

Patricia Byrd

Joy M. Reid

Cynthia M. Schuemann

Houghton Mifflin Company

Boston   New York

Publisher: Patricia A. Coryell
Director of ESL Publishing: Susan Maguire
Senior Development Editor: Kathy Sands Boehmer
Editorial Assistant: Evangeline Bermas
Senior Project Editor: Kathryn Dinovo
Manufacturing Assistant: Karmen Chong
Senior Marketing Manager: Annamarie Rice
Marketing Assistant: Andrew Whitacre

Cover graphics: LMA Communications, Natick, Massachusetts

Photo Credits: © Peter Beck/Corbis, p. 2; © Archivo Iconografico, S.A./Corbis, p. 4;
© Bettmann/Corbis, p. 16; © 2004 Banco de México Diego Rivera & Frida Kahlo Museums
Trust, p. 34; © Jose Luis Pelaez, Inc./Corbis, p. 46; © Jose Luis Pelaez, Inc./Corbis, p. 88;
© Roger Ressmeyer/Corbis, p. 88; © Royalty-Free/Corbis, p. 88; © Robert Holmes/Corbis,
p. 122; © 2000, The Washington Post Company, p. 124; © David Butow/Corbis SABA, p. 162.

2
College
Writing

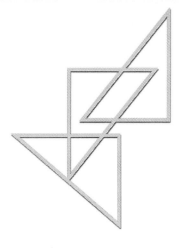

Contents

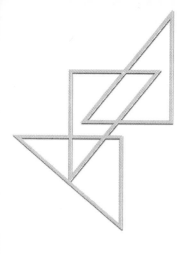

Houghton Mifflin English for Academic Success Series

SERIES EDITORS

Patricia Byrd, Joy M. Reid, Cynthia M. Schuemann

▷ What Is the Purpose of This Series?

The Houghton Mifflin English for Academic Success series is a comprehensive program of student and instructor materials: four levels of student language proficiency textbooks in three skill areas (oral communication, reading, and writing), with supplemental vocabulary textbooks at each level. For instructors and students, a useful website supports classroom teaching, learning and assessment. For instructors, four Essentials of Teaching Academic Language books (*Essentials of Teaching Academic Oral Communication, Essentials of Teaching Academic Reading, Essentials of Teaching Academic Writing*, and *Essentials of Teaching Academic Vocabulary*) provide helpful information for instructors new to teaching oral communication, reading, writing, and vocabulary.

The fundamental purpose of the series is to prepare students who are not native speakers of English for academic success in U.S. college degree programs. By studying these materials, students in college English for Academic Purposes (EAP) courses will gain the academic language skills they need to be successful students in degree programs. Additionally, students will learn about being successful students in U.S. college courses.

The series is based on considerable prior research as well as our own investigations of students' needs and interests, instructors' needs and desires, and institutional expectations and requirements. For example, our survey research revealed what problems instructors feel they face in their classrooms and what they actually teach; who the students are and what they know and do not know about the "culture" of U.S. colleges; and what types of exams are required for admission at various colleges.

Student Audience

The materials in this series are for college-bound ESL students at U.S. community colleges and undergraduate programs at other institutions. Some of these students are U.S. high school graduates. Some of them are long-term U.S. residents who graduated from a high school before coming to the United States. Others are newer U.S. residents. Still others are more typical international students. All of them need to develop academic language skills and knowledge of ways to be successful in U.S. college degree courses.

All of the books in this series have been created to implement the Houghton Mifflin English for Academic Success competencies. These competencies are based on those developed by ESL instructors and administrators in Florida, California, and Connecticut to be the underlying structure for EAP courses at colleges in those states. These widely respected competencies assure that the materials meet the real world needs of EAP students and instructors.

All of the books focus on . . .

► Starting where the students are, building on their strengths and prior knowledge (which is considerable, if not always academically relevant), and helping students self-identify needs and plans to strengthen academic language skills

► Academic English, including development of Academic Vocabulary and grammar required by students for academic speaking/listening, reading, and writing

► Master Student Skills, including learning style analysis, strategy training, and learning about the "culture" of U.S. colleges, which lead to their becoming successful students in degree courses and degree programs

► Topics and readings that represent a variety of academic disciplinary areas so that students learn about the language and content of the social sciences, the hard sciences, education, and business as well as the humanities

All of the books provide . . .

► Interesting and valuable content that helps the students develop their knowledge of academic content as well as their language skills and student skills

► A wide variety of practical classroom-tested activities that are easy to teach and engage the students

► Assessment tools at the end of each chapter so that instructors have easy-to-implement ways to assess student learning and students have opportunities to assess their own growth

► Websites for the students and for the instructors: the student sites will provide additional opportunities to practice reading, writing, listening, vocabulary development, and grammar. The instructor sites will provide instructors' manuals, teaching notes and answer keys, value-added materials like handouts and overheads that can be reproduced to use in class, and assessment tools such as additional tests to use beyond the assessment materials in each book.

▷ What Is the Purpose of the Writing Strand?

The Writing strand of the Houghton Mifflin English for Academic Success series prepares ESL students for academic written work, particularly in the first two years of college study. Many ESL students have learned English mostly through their ears; others have studied English primarily with their eyes. Each group has unique written-language problems. The goals of the writing books are to build on the strengths of the students, to respect the knowledge they have, and to identify and teach language, content, and rhetoric that students must have to succeed in college courses. The writing strategies presented focus on confidence building and step-by-step, easy-to-learn processes for effective academic writing.

The four writing textbooks prepare students for the range of writing tasks assigned in college courses, and the solid scaffolding of skills focus on "college culture" as well as on academic writing. The high-interest content-based chapters relate to academic work and college disciplines, and the chapter materials have been designed to appeal to a variety of student learning styles and strategies. The authentic native-English speaker (NES), ESL, and professional writing samples offer students examples of required writing in post-secondary institutions; the writing assignments have been drawn from actual college courses across the curriculum. In addition, the content of each textbook is based on the Houghton Mifflin Writing Competencies, which in turn are based on state-designed competencies developed by hundreds of experienced ESL instructors.

Grammar and Technology in the Writing Strand

Because the ESL population is so diverse in its grammar and rhetoric needs, each chapter contains Power Grammar boxes that introduce structures needed by the students to write fluent, accurate academic prose. The structures are drawn from the writing required by the chapter content. Students who need additional work with the structures are referred to the Houghton Mifflin website, where high-quality relevant additional support is available.

Assignments in the writing textbooks also ask students to use the Internet: to investigate topics and to identify and evaluate sources for research. Materials about citing sources is sequenced and spiraled through the books so that students exit the writing program with substantial practice with and knowledge about using sources.

Assessment Materials Accompanying the Writing Strand

This Writing strand is filled with informal and formal assessment. Students write, self-assess, and have significant opportunities for peer response and other external informal review, including instructor response. The end of each chapter contains additional writing tasks for practice or for testing/evaluation. Each chapter also asks students to self-evaluate the skills they have learned; these self-evaluations have proven surprisingly honest and accurate, and the results allow instructors to review and recycle necessary concepts. Finally, students regularly return to the revision process, revising even their "final" drafts after the papers are returned by the instructor, and receiving grades for those revisions.

More formally, the instructor website (http://esl.college.hmco.com/ instructors) and the *Essentials of Teaching Academic Writing* book offer assessment information and advice about both responding to and "grading" student writing. Information in these sources help instructors set up valid, reliable criteria for each student writing assignment in each book (which the instructors are encouraged to share with their students). These resources also contain sample student papers with instructor responses; sample topics to assess student strengths and weaknesses and to measure achievement and progress; and "benchmarked" student papers that describe the range of student grades.

Instructor Support Materials

The co-editors and Houghton Mifflin are committed to support instructors. For the Writing strand, the *Essentials of Teaching Academic Writing* by Joy Reid is an easily accessible, concise volume. This instructor resource, with its practical, problem-solving content, includes organizational suggestions for less experienced writing instructors, materials for response to and evaluation of student writing, and activities for teaching. In addition, each textbook has a password-protected website for instructors to provide classroom activities, substantial information and materials for assessment of student writing, and a "workbook" of printable pages linked to the textbook for use as handouts or overhead transparencies.

▷ What Is the Organization of *College Writing 2*?

College Writing 2 prepares intermediate students for success as academic writers. The five chapters work with paragraph length assignments to develop skill at academic writing based on different organizational patterns. Each writing assignment involves these three steps: Gathering Information, Focusing and Organizing, and Writing, Editing, and Revising. Topics are used that are of interest and relevance to college students and appropriate to academic courses that they will take. As they learn to collect and evaluate information to use in their writing, students practice critical thinking skills. *College Writing 2* helps students become aware of the differences between oral conversational language and written academic language. Students learn about many typical features of American college culture and instruction, including pair and group work, surveys, interviews, and case studies. The text begins with structured, guided writing activities but gradually removes the instructor from the process to help students become independent writers.

Chapter Organization

Each chapter has two to three writing assignments, in which the student is guided through a three-step writing process. The following common features appear in each chapter and support the writing process.

Spotlight on Writing Skills

Short explanations draw the student's attention to particular writing points that will be emphasized in the writing assignment and apply to successful academic writing.

Power Grammar

Each chapter provides a quick review or teaching point that is pertinent to that chapter's writing assignments. The Power Grammar exercises allow students to self-evaluate and instructors to determine if additional work is necessary. Two to four grammar points are presented, based on and integrated into the writing assignments.

Web Power

Web Power is a feature that reminds students that additional resources for practice of grammar points are provided online.

Graphic Organizers

Students learn to use graphic organizers to aid in writing and critical thinking.

Self-Editing and Peer Response

All writing assignments include self-editing and peer response exercises, using peer response sheets from the appendix.

Master Student Tips

These tips offer quick bites of information to help students become better college students.

Editing Cards

In Chapter 1, students begin editing cards based on their own individual needs and update them as they progress through assignments.

Sample Paragraphs

Each chapter contains student writing samples for comparison, analysis, and discussion.

Reflection, Self-Evaluation, and Instructor Assessment of Student Writing

Each chapter ends with additional topics for practice and assessment, as well as reflection activities, giving students and the instructor an opportunity to assess mastery of key points taught in the chapter and to apply the critical thinking skills presented in each chapter.

Acknowledgments

My thanks to all those who have supported me throughout this project. At Houghton Mifflin, special thanks to ESL editor Susan Maguire and developmental editor Kathy Sands Boehmer for their steadfast faith in the series. My profound thanks to our series editors, Pat Byrd, Cynthia Schuemann, and especially to Joy Reid, my primary editor. They helped me bring this book to life through their coaching and coaxing.

My faculty advisors, Lindy Daubin, Karen Miller, Karen Trebilcock, Samir Latif, Kay Douglas, generously read the drafts, tried out the materials and gave me great advice.

My students gave me essential feedback on the content of the book. Their perspective guided all my revisions. I especially thank the following students who permitted me to use their writing in the book: Urmi Kotadia, Andre Margutti, Hanna Worku, Kevin Choi, Rossangela Lastaria, Erick Paul Salas, Jin Goo Kang, Marijane Maglaque, Karina Castillo, Thao Phan, Kim Leggiero, Rose Gomes, Shreyash M. Upadhyaya, and Antonia Cruz.

I also thank the reviewers who contributed tremendously to my understanding of how to construct a textbook:

Linda Choi, Canada College
Katherine Crawford, American River College
Kathy Flynn, Glendale Community College
Diane Kraemer, Hillsborough Community College
Denise Marceaux, University of Louisiana, Lafayette
Maria Marin, DeAnza College
Patricia McGee, Camden County College
Jackie Pena, Northern Essex Community College
Mary Ann Raimond, Sussex County Community College
Margaret Redus, Richmond College
Michelle Schweitzer, Bunker Hill Community College
Richard Skinner, Hudson County Community College
Christine Tierney, Houston Community College
Bob Underwood, American River College
Elizabeth Winkler, University of Arizona
and Sharon Wood, Clackamas Community College.

Finally, my most sincere thanks to my friends and family who consistently buoyed me through the long months of writing and revising, particularly my husband, John, who could not have been more encouraging.

▷ What Student Competencies Are Covered in *College Writing 2*?

Description of Overall Purposes

Students continue to develop academic writing with an emphasis on writing level-appropriate academic paragraphs in the traditional modes: observing, describing, informing, explaining processes and/or classifying, and explaining cause(s) and/or effect(s).

Materials in this textbook are designed with the following minimum exit objectives in mind:

Competency 1:
(level/global focus)
The student will compose a variety of paragraphs of varying lengths about academic topics, ending with writing multiple paragraphs on a single topic.

Competency 2:
(critical thinking)
The student will enhance the ability to distinguish between main ideas and supporting information/ details/examples in their written texts.

Competency 3:
(organization)
The student will practice the overall and inner paragraph organization of the traditional academic paragraph modes, including chronological, spatial, and most-to-least important organization.

Competency 4:
(grammar)
The student will write accurate Standard English appropriate to the level, and the student will practice proofreading and editing grammar and sentence structure appropriate to the level.

Competency 5:
(research skills)
The student will enhance development in use of the Internet for academic purposes: to gather materials and cite those materials appropriately.

Competency 6:
(critical thinking)
The student will develop interview questions and interview resources to support the written information; the student will cite the interview source appropriately.

Competency 7:
(critical thinking)
The student will continue to develop sensitivity and practice the necessary skills for analyzing audience and purpose in academic writing.

Competency 8:
(critical thinking)

The student will develop the following critical thinking skills when writing. The student will:

A. analyze the academic and audience related reasons for using the traditional "modal" patterns of organization;

B. learn and practice basic academic (APA) citation methods for interviews;

C. discuss and understand the philosophy of presenting written materials with a purpose (means and ends);

D. analyze academic cultural phenomenon through writing;

E. apply content knowledge to academic tasks (e.g., test-taking, interacting with academic culture, reading and analyzing academic sources).

Competency 9:
(culture)

The student will recognize, investigate, write about, and discuss common academic cultural references.

Competency 10:
(study strategies)

The student will enhance awareness of study skills, learning styles, and strategies necessary when writing for academic purposes.

▷ **What Are the Features of the Writing Books?**

The Houghton Mifflin English for Academic Success series is a comprehensive program of student and instructor materials. The fundamental purpose of the program is to prepare students who are not native speakers of English for academic success in U.S. college degree programs.

The Writing strand of the Houghton Mifflin English for Academic Success series focuses on the development of writing skills and general background knowledge necessary for college study. Dedicated to meeting academic needs of students by teaching them how to handle the writing demands and expectations of college-level classes, the goals of the writing books are to build on the strengths of the students, to respect the knowledge they have, and to identify and teach language, content, and rhetoric that students must have to succeed in college courses.

Academic Content: The content of each book relates to academic subjects and has been selected because of its high interest for students and because of the popularity of these particular disciplines/courses on college campuses.

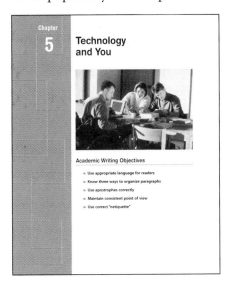

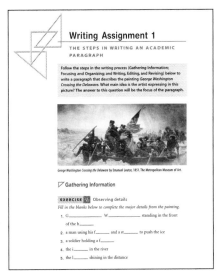

Authentic Writing Assignments: The writing assignments have been drawn from actual college courses across the curriculum. Students will find the assignments highly motivating when they realize they may receive such an assignment in one of their future classes.

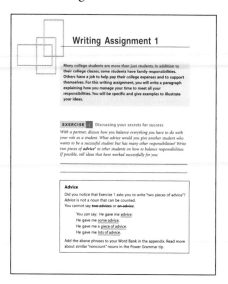

Authentic Writing Models: Models provide specific examples of student writing so that students can compare writing styles, discuss writing strategies and understand instructor expectations.

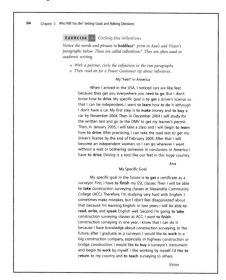

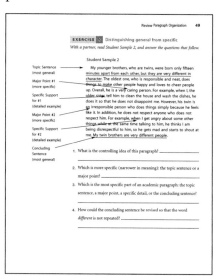

Step-by-Step Writing Process: The step-by-step writing process helps demystify the concept of "academic writing" and helps students develop confidence. The textbooks offer solid scaffolding of skills that focus on college culture as well as on academic topics and academic writing. These are supplemented by practical advice offered in the Spotlight on Writing Skills feature boxes.

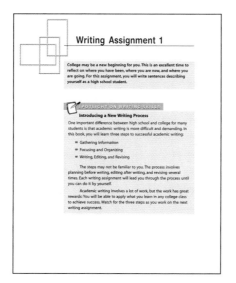

Self-Assessment Opportunity: A writing course develops through assessment. Students write and revise and instructors respond and evaluate and then students write some more. The textbooks offer students opportunity for peer response, self-review, and self-evaluation.

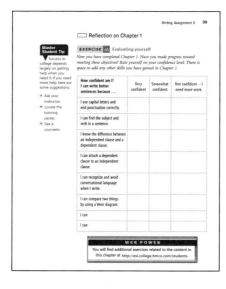

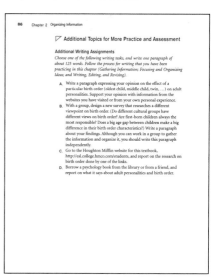

Master Student Tips: Master Student Tips throughout the textbooks provide students with short comments on a particular strategy, activity, or practical advice to follow in an academic setting.

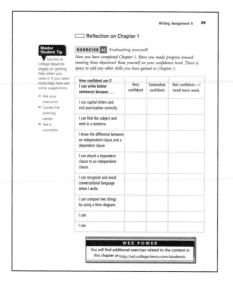

Power Grammar Boxes: Students can be very diverse in their grammar and rhetorical needs, so each chapter contains Power Grammar boxes that introduce grammar structures students need to be fluent and accurate in academic English.

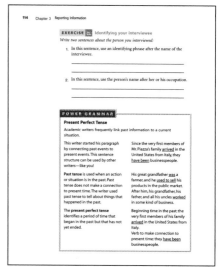

Ancillary Program: The ancillary program provides instructors with teaching tips, additional exercises, and robust assessment. Students can also take advantage of additional exercises and activities. The following items are available to accompany the Houghton Mifflin English for Academic Success series Writing strand:

- ▶ Instructor website: Additional teaching materials, activities, and robust student assessment.
- ▶ Student website: Additional exercises, activities, and web links.
- ▶ The Houghton Mifflin English for Academic Success series Vocabulary books: You can choose the appropriate level to shrinkwrap with your text.
- ▶ Option to use the SMARTHINKING live online tutoring service which will answer grammar questions. Students can also take unlimited advantage of the Online Writing Lab, which will provide them with detailed feedback on how to improve their paragraphs.
- ▶ The *Essentials of Teaching Academic Writing* by Joy M. Reid is available for purchase. It gives you theoretical and practical information for teaching writing.

1

Writing Descriptions

An artist's portrait of a person is more than a photograph. The painted portrait reveals what the artist believed was important about that person. Look at the portraits in the picture above. What is the artist saying about these people? What specific details from the portraits reveal the artist's ideas and attitude?

Chapter Objectives

In this chapter, you will write at least two descriptive paragraphs. While completing these paragraphs you will:	I have learned this well.	I need to work on this.
Learn the three steps in the writing process		
Construct an outline to organize your ideas		
Use correct paragraph format		
Write topic sentences with clear controlling ideas		
Fully develop details in supporting sentences		
Write concluding sentences		
Distinguish between clauses and phrases		
Recognize sentences		
Use adjectives and adjective clauses to improve your descriptive writing		
Become aware of the importance of verb endings in academic writing		
Edit paragraphs for format, punctuation, and subject/verb agreement		

Paragraph Organization and Format

In this book, you will learn to write academic paragraphs. The first things we will go over are the format (how a paragraph looks) and the organization (how the ideas and information are put together) of an academic paragraph.

EXERCISE 1 Discussing as a class

What do you know about George Washington and the American Revolution? Use the questions in the boxes around the picture to guide a discussion. List vocabulary words on the board.

Who is the man in this painting?

When was the Revolutionary War?

Why is this man wearing a wig?

Does this painting show this man before or after the Revolutionary War?

Who was on either side of the Revolutionary War?

What job did this man have at the time shown in the painting? What about before this time?

George Washington by Gilbert Stuart, 1796. National Portrait Gallery, Smithsonian Institution.

EXERCISE 2 Learning more about George Washington

Do some research to learn more about George Washington.

Visit the Houghton Mifflin website for this textbook at http://esl.college.hmco.com/students for a listing of websites that discuss George Washington, the American Revolution, and paintings of the first President, or type in the keywords George Washington *and* American Revolution *in a search engine.*

OR

Go the library and look up George Washington *or* American Revolution *in a reference book.*

Take notes on one of the forms below.

Site Name: _____

URL: _____

Date visited: _____

New or interesting information:

Title: _____

Author/Publisher: _____

Date of publication: _____

New or interesting information:

Report back to the class at least two new or interesting facts that you found.

EXERCISE 3 Freewriting

Freewriting is a way to brainstorm ideas while developing fluency in writing. Freewriting is never scored or corrected. It is free of rules and expectations. You just spend a few minutes writing down anything that comes into your mind about a subject. The important thing is to continue writing. If you can't think of anything to write, write about how you can't think of anything to write. Remember, freewriting is a writing warm-up activity, so just like you should warm-up before doing real exercises, spend time freewriting before you try to write academic paragraphs. Also like physical activities, you will get better at freewriting with practice. Enjoy it!

For this writing assignment, spend five minutes writing about George Washington and the American Revolution.

▶ Write any ideas that come to you about the topic.
▶ Write as much as you can without stopping.
▶ Put all your ideas down on paper.
▶ Do not worry about making mistakes.
▶ Do not worry about spelling, punctuation, organization, or grammar.
▶ Just write and don't stop for five minutes.

EXERCISE 4 Reading a student sample[1]

Read Student Sample 1 and notice the shape and the content of the paragraph.

Student Sample 1

Topic Sentence with Controlling Idea

Four Major Supporting Details with specific supporting details/ analysis for each

Concluding Sentence

    In this painting, the artist shows George Washington, who was the first president of the United States, as a confident leader. The expression on his face is firm and not afraid. His right hand is welcoming people to join the new country. His left hand is holding a sword, which shows that he was ready to protect his new government. He is standing in front of giant pillars that represent strength and power. The artist is showing President Washington had been a great soldier during the Revolutionary War and now he was ready and able to lead the new country.

1. Student Samples are finished paragraphs, not freewriting examples.

EXERCISE 5   Recognizing correct paragraph format

Look at Student Sample 1 and notice the shape. Paragraphs have a particular shape or format. The first line is indented (the first line begins slightly to the right), and all other lines go from margin to margin (about an inch from either side). The last line may end before the margin. Most published writings have even margins on both sides. Handwritten paragraphs usually have a slightly uneven right margin.

Xxxx xx xxxx. *Xxxx xxxx xxxxxx,* *xxx xxxxxxx. Xxxx* *xxxxx xxx xx. Xxxx* *xxxxxxx, xx xxxxx* *xxx. Xx xxxxxx xx,* *xxx xxxx xxxx xx* *xxxxx. Xxxxxx, xxx* *xx x xxxx xxxx xxx* *xxx. Xxx xxx xxxx.* *Xxx xx.*	*Xxxx xx xxxx. Xxxx* *xxxx, xxxxx xxxx,* *xxx xxxxxxx. Xxxx* *xxxxxxx, Xxx xxxxx* *xx,* *xx. Xxxxxx xxxxxx.* *Xxxxxx, xxx xx x* *xxxx xxxx xxx xxxx.* *Xxx xxx xx xx xxx* *xxxxx. Xxxxxx, xxx* *xx x xxxx xxxx xxx.*	*Xxxx xx xxxxx.* *Xxxx xxxx xxxxxx* *xxx xxxxxx. Xxxx* *xxxxx xxx xx.* *Xxxx xxxxxxx,* *xxxxx xxx. Xxxx* *xxxxxx xx, xxx xxxx* *xxxx xx xxxx. Xxxx* *Xxxxxx,* *xxxx xxxx xxx xxx* *xxx xxxxx.*
1.	2.	3.

Which of the boxes shows one paragraph with correct paragraph format?

_____

Each of the other boxes has two errors in paragraph format. What are they?

_____

_____

_____

_____

_____

EXERCISE 6   **Recognizing paragraph content**

In a paragraph, the sentence that expresses the controlling idea about the topic is called the topic sentence. In the topic sentence, one or more words express this main idea. This main idea is called the controlling idea because it controls the information that will be in the rest of the paragraph. The other sentences contain information that explains, clarifies, or describes this one main idea. These sentences contain the details that support the topic sentence. The final sentence in a paragraph is frequently a concluding sentence.

*Reread Student Sample 1. The topic sentence is in **bold**. The controlling idea is underlined. The next sentences contain the major details that support this topic sentence. They are underlined.*

Fill in the blanks in the box below with information from Student Sample 1:

Topic Sentence: _____

_____

_____

Controlling Idea: _____

_____

_____

    Major Detail #1: _____

    Major Detail #2: _____

    Major Detail #3: _____

    Major Detail #4: _____

EXERCISE 7   Choosing a topic sentence

Choose the best topic sentence for the short paragraphs below. Underline the supporting information in each short paragraph for the topic sentence's controlling idea.

1. _____. The marble pillars represent power and strength. He is holding a sword that shows his military might. The clouds indicate trouble, and the curtains are blowing and twisting, but George Washington is not affected.

   a. The picture is about George Washington, who was the first president of the United States.
   b. The picture shows George Washington as a strong and powerful leader.

2. _____. He is gesturing with his right hand to welcome people into his office. He is dressed nicely but simply. He does not wear a crown or a robe. The chair behind him is made of wood with a seal of the United States on the back.

   a. The artist showed that George Washington was a man of the people and not a king.
   b. The artist showed that George Washington was a powerful man who was willing to protect the new country.

3. _____. The president is facing forward, toward the future. His hand is extended in a welcoming, not threatening, gesture. The clouds and wind, which represent a big storm or a difficult time, are behind him.

   a. This picture shows the hopefulness that the people of the United States had after the Revolutionary War.
   b. George Washington is not dressed in a military uniform.

EXERCISE 8   Locating a topic sentence and details

Read Student Sample 2.

Student Sample 2

> In this picture, the artist showed the strength of America and its people. George Washington is standing tall and erect. The curtains behind him are blowing in the strong winds, but he is not moving. He is holding a sword, which shows that he is able to protect the country. Tall marble pillars are behind him. These have been symbols of strong governments for many centuries. The chair next to George Washington is sturdy and solid. The Declaration of Independence is on the massive table.

Underline the topic sentence.

Number the major supporting details that explain, clarify, or describe the topic sentence.

POWER GRAMMAR

Verbs and Clauses

Every clause must contain a verb.

Verbs show time. Different times are shown by using different verb tense markings.	…the artist **shows** … …the artist **showed** … Tall marble pillars **are** … … Washington **had been** …
Verbs have **subjects**. Locate the subject by asking *Who?* or *What?* in front of the verb. The answer is the subject.	…**the artist** shows …(Who shows?) …**the artist** showed …(Who showed?) **Tall marble pillars** are …(What are?) …**Washington** had been … (Who had been?)
Phrases are groups of words without a subject and verb.	…in front of giant pillars … …the strength of America and its people …
Clauses are groups of words with a subject and verb.	…**who was** the first president of the United States … **His left hand is holding** a sword.

EXERCISE 9   **Recognizing clauses**

Write a C in front of the clauses. Write an X in front of the phrases.

Example:

___*C*___   He is standing

___*X*___   The hand-carved chair with a shield of the United States on the back

1. _____   The rug on the floor and the curtains behind him

2. _____   Marble columns have been symbols of power and stability for centuries

3. _____   To welcome newcomers to this country

4. _____   When the United States government began to function

5. _____   His outfit is typical of formal clothing of that time period

6. _____   The book under the wooden table

7. _____   Who signed the Declaration of Independence

8. _____   The curtain behind him

9. _____   Tall pillars are behind him

EXERCISE 10   **Explaining your choices**

With a partner, go over Exercise 9 and write down the number of the choices that are not clauses. Explain why each is not a clause.

#_____ because _____

#_____ because _____

#_____ because _____

#_____ because _____

EXERCISE 11   Locating clauses

Complete the activities in the four sentences below.

Read each sentence.

Underline each verb, and circle each subject.

Count the number of clauses in each sentence, and write the number on the line next to the sentence.

1. _____ The picture shows George Washington as a strong and powerful leader.

2. _____ The marble pillars represent power and strength.

3. _____ He is holding a sword that shows his military might.

4. _____ The clouds indicate trouble, and the curtains are blowing and twisting, but George Washington is not affected.

EXERCISE 12   Checking your answers

Check your answers with a partner. If you disagree, check with another pair of partners.

POWER GRAMMAR

Independent and Dependent Clauses

Independent clauses can stand alone. Dependent clauses must be connected to an independent clause.

A clause that expresses a complete thought is an **independent clause**.	The United States formed a new government.
A **dependent clause** is a clause that must be attached to an independent clause in order to complete a thought.	When the Revolutionary War ended. (This only tells the time when something happened. It does not tell a complete thought.)
A **sentence** is a clause or group of clauses that expresses a complete thought.	When the Revolutionary War ended, the United States formed a new government.

EXERCISE 13   Recognizing sentences

Review the following clauses. Put a period at the end of each sentence
(a clause or group of clauses that expresses a complete thought). Be careful:
Not all the clauses are sentences.

1. George Washington was a farmer
2. If England won the war
3. Which is on the table
4. The Declaration of Independence is now on display in the National Archives
5. The chair that is behind him is made of wood
6. Which shows that he is able to protect the country
7. Virginia was one of the thirteen colonies

EXERCISE 14   Explaining your answers

With a partner, go over Exercise 13 and write down the number of each
group of words that is <u>not</u> a sentence. Then explain why these are <u>not</u>
sentences.

#_____ because _____

#_____ because _____

#_____ because _____

EXERCISE 15   Checking your answers

Check your answers with another pair of partners.

EXERCISE 16 Combining clauses

Select a dependent clause from the box below and write it next to the correct independent clause (numbered below).

---

during the Revolutionary War
before the Revolutionary War
because the British king would not permit the colonies freedom
who was from Virginia

---

1. _____, the American colonies did not have an army.

2. _____, George Washington was the commander-in-chief of the American army.

3. George Washington, _____, became the first president of the new country.

4. The Declaration of Independence was written _____

   _____.

EXERCISE 17 Checking your answers

Check your answers with a partner. If you disagree, check with another pair of partners.

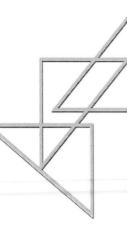

Writing Assignment 1

THE STEPS IN WRITING AN ACADEMIC PARAGRAPH

Follow the steps in the writing process (Gathering Information; Focusing and Organizing; and Writing, Editing, and Revising) below to write a paragraph that describes the painting *George Washington Crossing the Delaware*. What main idea is the artist expressing in this picture? The answer to this question will be the focus of the paragraph.

George Washington Crossing the Delaware by Emanuel Leutze, 1851. The Metropolitan Museum of Art.

▷ Gathering Information

EXERCISE 18 Observing details

Fill in the blanks below to complete the major details from the painting.

1. G_____ W_____ standing in the front of the b____

2. a man using his f____ and a st____ to push the ice

3. a soldier holding a f____

4. the i____ in the river

5. the l____ shining in the distance

EXERCISE 19   Discussing as a class

With your classmates, discuss what you think is going on in the painting. What is about to happen? How do you think the soldiers feel? Do you think George Washington really stood like this in the boat? Why did the artist paint the light in the background? How does that make you feel about what is going to happen?

▷ Focusing and Organizing

EXERCISE 20   Developing a main idea

With a small group of classmates, discuss what you think the artist was trying to say in this picture. Develop a sentence that expresses the overall idea of the artist. (This is a "working" topic sentence. You may change or improve it later.)

> **Example:** The artist seems to be saying that George Washington bravely led his men into battle.

EXERCISE 21   Focusing the details

Think about taking a photograph. You look through the camera's viewfinder and see a large scene. Then you focus the camera on a few flowers that are very near. You decide the flowers are what you really want to capture and remember. Of course, you lose the larger scene, but the focus on the flowers makes an interesting and beautiful photo. Similarly, you focus a paragraph by "narrowing" the focus to fit the assignment, the audience, and/or the available information. A focused paragraph is more interesting to a reader. One way to narrow the focus is to decide which details are (or are not) directly related to the topic.

Review the details from the painting, and cross out the one detail that is the least related to the main idea of the artist:

1. George Washington standing in the front of the boat
2. a man using his foot and a stick to push the ice
3. a soldier holding a flag
4. the ice in the river
5. the light shining in the distance

EXERCISE 22 Discussing your answer

With a partner, discuss why you eliminated the detail that you chose.

SPOTLIGHT ON WRITING SKILLS

Descriptive Writing

An artist expresses ideas with paint. A writer expresses ideas with words. The artist's details are carefully chosen and painted. Similarly, the writer must carefully choose words that let the reader "see" the visual details.

> The man is standing.

This is a sentence, but not a very descriptive one. If you add words that describe details in the picture, readers can "see" the picture without having the painting in front of them.

> The strong man, who is dressed in a general's uniform, is standing in the front of a small, crowded boat that is crossing an icy river.

Your goal when writing academic paragraphs is to write powerful, interesting sentences that express your ideas in an organized way. One way to add interest to your sentences is to use adjectives and adjective clauses.

POWER GRAMMAR

Adjectives and Adjective Clauses

Adding descriptive information to your details will make your writing more interesting and more powerful.

A word that describes something is an **adjective**.	*The **strong** man is standing in the front of a **small, crowded** boat.*
A clause that describes something is an **adjective clause**.	*The strong man, **who is dressed in a general's uniform**, is standing in the front of a small, crowded boat **that is crossing an icy river**.*

(Continued)

An adjective clause usually (but not always) begins with a pronoun that substitutes for the noun that is being described.

*The strong **man**, **who** is dressed in a general's uniform, is standing in the front of a small, crowded **boat that** is crossing an icy river.*

The most important of these pronouns are *who*, *that*, and *which*.
- ► *who* substitutes for people
- ► *that* substitutes for things (and sometimes for people)
- ► *which* substitutes for things

The army is crossing a river which is full of ice.

The information in the adjective clause, while informative and interesting, is not the most important information in the sentence. Since this is the topic sentence of a paragraph that analyzes the painting, the information about the artist's view of George Washington is more important.

In this painting, the artist shows George Washington as a confident leader. He was the first president of the United States.

In this painting, the artist shows George Washington, who was the first president of the United States, as a confident leader.

(This topic sentence is from a paragraph about Washington's strength and confidence. That is the important information.)

A special use of a *which* clause is to describe an entire idea, not just the one noun. This is frequently used in conversational speech. Although it is also acceptable in academic writing, it can sometimes be confusing.

George Washington is standing in the front of the small boat, which shows that he was the leader of the army.

(The adjective clause is describing the entire idea, not just the word *boat*.)

When the *which* clause is describing an entire idea, the clause comes at the end. A comma is used to separate the adjective clause from the rest of the sentence.

EXERCISE 23   Developing your vocabulary

With a partner, fill in the chart with adjectives that describe the details of the painting. Use a dictionary or a thesaurus to help find adjectives that are vivid, not boring.

George Washington	
flag	
river	
light	
boat	*crowded, small, undersized, dangerous, precarious*

EXERCISE 24   Locating adjective clauses

Underline the adjective clauses. Circle the word being described.

> **Example:** Next to George Washington is a soldier who is holding an American flag.

1. The boat is being steered by a man who is in the rear of the boat.

2. The flag that the soldier is holding is red, white, and blue.

3. The light, which is shining in the distance, represents success.

4. This painting, which portrays the beginning of the Battle of Trenton in 1776, was done by Emanuel Leutze, who painted it in 1851.

EXERCISE 25 Connecting adjective clauses to their nouns

The adjective clauses in the sentences below describe a person or object in the painting George Washington Crossing the Delaware. *Fill in the blanks with the correct noun.*

1. The _____ who are sitting in the boat look cold.

2. George Washington is standing in a _____, which is small and crowded.

3. The _____ who is holding the flag is standing next to _____, who is looking stright ahead.

4. The _____, which is filled with ice, represents the difficult struggles that the American army faced during the Revolutionary War.

EXERCISE 26 Placing adjectives and adjective clauses

In the painting, the artist put the ice in the river, not on General Washington. When he wanted to show the general's uniform, he painted it on the general, not on the soldier steering the boat. In the same way, when you are creating your written picture by adding specific details, put the details in the right place.

1. Where are adjectives located? _____

_____

_____

_____

2. Where are adjective clauses located? _____

_____

_____

_____

EXERCISE 27 Combining sentences using adjective clauses

Join the pairs of sentences by using an adjective clause.

Example:

The painting is owned by the National Gallery of Art.
The National Gallery of Art is in Washington, D.C.

The painting is owned by the National Gallery of Art, which is in Washington, D.C.

1. The artist also painted portraits of other American heroes.
   The artist painted several portraits of George Washington.

   _____

   _____

2. The Battle of Trenton occurred on December 26, 1776.
   Trenton is a city in New Jersey.

   _____

   _____

3. Before the Revolutionary War, George Washington was a farmer.
   George Washington lived in Virginia.

   _____

   _____

4. After the Revolutionary War, the colonies became independent.
   The Revolutionary War lasted seven years.

   _____

   _____

EXERCISE 28 Locating adjectives and adjective clauses

Reread Student Sample 1 (p. 7). Underline the three adjective clauses and five of the adjectives.

EXERCISE 29   Using adjective clauses to clarify ideas

Refer to Student Sample 2 (p. 11) to answer the following questions.

Student Sample 2 contains these two sentences: *Tall marble pillars are behind him. These have been symbols of strong governments for many centuries.* Join these sentences by making one of them an adjective clause. This will show the connection between the ideas more clearly.

_____

_____

Student Sample 2 also contains this sentence: *The Declaration of Independence is on the massive table.* Add an adjective clause to clarify how this detail is connected to the main idea of the paragraph.

_____

_____

WEB POWER

Visit the website for this text at
http://esl.college.hmco.com/students for sites that can
help you practice adjective clauses.

SPOTLIGHT ON WRITING SKILLS

Develop Your Details

There are many details in the painting, but your paragraph should only contain details that support your main idea.

Because you cannot ask the artist why he chose certain details or exactly what he meant by the details, you must try to analyze them yourself. Of course, you cannot be 100 percent sure what the artist meant. However, you can make **inferences** based on what you see in the painting. Inferences are educated guesses or logical conclusions. Different students might make different inferences, but all students should be able to explain their inferences.

EXERCISE 30 **Determining the meaning of details**

Fill in the chart to explain the meaning or the importance of the details in the painting. The first one has been done for you, but you may add more ideas or change the ideas if you wish.

Details from the painting	Meaning
George Washington standing in the front of the boat	*That shows he is the leader. The boat looks small and scary, but he looks brave. It shows that the Americans will win the battle.*
flag	
ice in the river	
light	
boat	

WEB POWER

Visit the website for this text at
http://esl.college.hmco.com/students to learn
more about graphic organizers.

SPOTLIGHT ON WRITING SKILLS

Graphic Organizers

Graphic organizers are visuals that show the relationships between ideas. Dozens of different types of graphic organizers are used in college, including maps, diagrams, and flow charts. You will use timelines in history classes, diagrams in biology lab reports, and flow charts in computer programming classes.

Writers in all subject areas frequently use graphic organizers to organize their ideas before they write a paragraph or paper. A traditional graphic organizer in academic work is an outline, which we will use for this assignment. An outline organizes information by starting with the most general ideas and moving toward more specific items. By using indentations, an outline clearly shows the different levels of the information. It also shows which supporting information goes together so that the writer can easily transfer this logical organization to her or his paragraph.

Outline Format

[The main idea is written on the top.]

I. First Major Supporting Detail
  A. Specific Supporting Detail
  B. Specific Supporting Detail
    1. Most Specific Supporting Detail
    2. Most Specific Supporting Detail

II. Second Major Supporting Detail
  A. Specific Supporting Detail
    1. Most Specific Supporting Deail
    2. Most Specific Supporting Detail
  B. Specific Supporting Detail
  C. Specific Supporting Detail
    1. Most Specific Supporting Detail
    2. Most Specific Supporting Detail
    3. Most Specific Supporting Detail

III. Third Major Supporting Detail
  A. Specific Supporting Detail

IV. Conclusion

EXERCISE 31   Analyzing outline format

With a partner, use the outline format on the previous page to answer these questions.

1. How many major supporting details will be in this paragraph?

    _____

2. How many specific supporting details support the second major point?

    _____

3. How many specific supporting details support the conclusion?

    _____

4. What do you think I, B, 2 refers to?

    _____

5. In the final paragraph, which major supporting detail will have the most specific supporting details?

    _____

6. How many times is the main idea stated?

    _____

7. Why is there no number "1" or "2" for the third major detail?

    _____

    _____

8. Do you think outlines would help <u>you</u> organize your writing? Why or why not?

    _____

    _____

    _____

EXERCISE 32 **Constructing an outline**

Complete the outline below with the major supporting details and specific supporting details from the chart on page 24. You can leave out some details if you think they are not important or interesting. You may have several specific details for one of the major details and only one specific detail for another. The details that you select may differ slightly from another student's choices.

Also write down why the details you choose to include support the main idea of the paragraph. Each student may see a different meaning in the details. However, each student must be able to explain why the details support the main idea of the paragraph.

The organization of the ideas in the paragraphs will reflect the visual organization of the outlines that you produce. Your sentences describing and explaining the specific details about the figure of George Washington will come immediately after the sentence that states the major detail of George Washington. You would not write a sentence explaining how the river looks in the middle of the sentences describing the figure of George Washington.

Main Idea:

> **Example:** The artist is saying that George Washington bravely led his men into battle.

_____

_____

I. George Washington
    A. he is standing in front of the boat and looking ahead
       1. this shows he is brave
       2. this shows he is the leader
    B. he is wearing a general's uniform
       1. this also shows he is the leader

II. flag

III. ice in the river

IV. light

V. boat

▷ Writing, Editing, and Revising

EXERCISE 33 Writing your first draft

Write the first draft of your paragraph. Be sure to indent the first line and to write from margin to margin. Use your outline to construct your paragraph. Begin with your topic sentence, and add sentences that give major details and specific supporting details.

SPOTLIGHT ON WRITING SKILLS

Concluding Sentences

A paragraph should not just stop abruptly. It should bring your thoughts to a conclusion. A conclusion for a paragraph can serve many different functions, some of which follow:

- ► Restate the main idea
- ► Ask for a response
- ► Evaluate the topic
- ► Make a suggestion
- ► State a prediction
- ► Link to another paragraph

EXERCISE 34 Developing concluding sentences

Use Student Samples 1 and 2 to answer these questions.

Reread Student Sample 1 (p. 7), and underline the concluding sentence. What function does this concluding sentence serve?

Reread Student Sample 2 (p. 11). It has no concluding sentence. As a class, decide what a good concluding sentence for this sample might be. Write it on the board.

EXERCISE 35 Writing a concluding sentence

Reread your own paragraph and add a concluding sentence.

"Eye" Learners and "Ear" Learners

Some English as a Second Language (ESL) students learn English primarily with their eyes. That is, they study English in textbooks and learn the grammar and vocabulary of English before they speak the language. These "eye" learners may understand the rules of English grammar well, but they may have some difficulty speaking the language fluently.

Many other students are "ear" learners. That is, they have learned English primarily through their ears, by listening to the language—with friends, on television, at school. However, this spoken English is not exactly the same as written English, especially <u>formal academic written English</u>. In college, students must be able to understand and produce formal academic written English.

One area of confusion for ear learners is the difference between how words are spoken and how they are written. For example, *He is going to go to the museum* can sometimes sound like *Heez gonna go ta the museum.*

In English, the endings of verbs are very important. As you reviewed on page 12, in English, verbs always indicate time (also called *tense*). For example, sometimes a verb will end in *-ed* to show past time (or *past tense*). Other verbs will end in *-ing* to show an action in progress. Some verbs are irregular, which means that the verb's spelling is changed when the tense changes.

Unfortunately for ear learners, these endings and spelling changes are usually not emphasized when a person is speaking, so a listener might not notice the important endings or spelling changes. If ear learners write what they hear, the writing will be incorrect and confusing to readers. In academic writing, accuracy and clarity are always important, so ear learners of English must learn to self-correct these errors.

Master Student Tip

▼Use a dictionary (paper or electronic) to check the spelling of irregular verbs. For instance, it is difficult to hear the difference between *begin, began,* and *begun.*

You can also use a dictionary to prevent spelling errors when you are adding endings onto verbs. There is a big difference between *hoping* and *hopping.*

EXERCISE 36 Hearing "Whaddya Say?"

What we hear is not always what we write!

Complete the words used in the sentences your instructor reads aloud.

1. Before the exhibit be _____ , the artist was ho _____ to complet _____ a final piece of sculpture.

2. The artist pain _____ a portrait recently even though she usually pain _____ pictures of landscapes.

3. The students who w _____ to the gallery opening ha _____ ha _____ no previous experience describ _____ artwork.

4. When he w _____ a child, my brother lik _____ to collec _____ postage stamps which sho _____ famous paintings.

5. My cousin ho _____ to g _____ a degree in fine arts, which is the same degree that his mother g _____ when she stud _____ here a few years ago.

6. The artist who w _____ at the museum last night i _____ travel _____ to Mexico soon.

7. The painters who w _____ exhibi _____ in the gallery might ear _____ a lot of money.

W E B   P O W E R

Visit the College Writing 2 website for this textbook at
http://esl.college.hmco.com/students for a listing of
irregular verbs.

EXERCISE 37   Editing your paragraph

Review your paragraph.

Underline each verb, and circle each subject.

Fill in the chart to make sure each verb is written in the correct tense.

Verb	Tense	Why did you choose this tense?

Make sure you have begun every sentence with a CAPITAL letter and completed every sentence with a period.

Make sure each adjective is in front of its noun and each adjective clause is immediately after its noun.

Rewrite your paragraph.

EXERCISE 38   Reviewing a classmate's paragraph

Exchange your textbook and your paragraph with another student. Use the form below in your partner's textbook to check your partner's paragraph for proper format, capitalization, and ending punctuation. Read the paragraph to see if the content is clear. Add any comments that you think would help the student improve the paragraph.

Peer Reader's Name: _____

Is the paragraph properly formatted?   Yes / No
Do all the sentences begin with a capital letter and
end with a period?   Yes / No
Do all the clauses have a subject and a verb?   Yes / No

Write down two subject-verb combinations _____
Do all the detail sentences support the topic sentence?   Yes / No
Is the information clear to you?   Yes / No

Comments? _____

EXERCISE 39   Revising your paragraph

Reread your paragraph.

Consider the comments made by your partner. What changes can you make to improve your paragraph?

Think of what you saw in your partner's paragraph. Did you learn anything from reviewing your partner's paragraph that could help improve your paragraph?

What other improvements can you make? Do you want to add more specific details? Do you want to change the order of the sentences or combine some sentences?

Rewrite your paragraph, and submit your paragraph to your instructor.

EXERCISE 40 Rewriting your paragraph

When you receive your paragraph back from your instructor, rewrite it as necessary.

SPOTLIGHT ON WRITING SKILLS

Folders

Keep all your drafts and final paragraphs in a folder. At the end of the semester, you and your instructor will be able to review your progress in writing. Perhaps you will want to rewrite some of your early paragraphs at the end of the semester.

This folder can be used as a portfolio in which you can collect not only your finished paragraphs but also other types of writing that you do during the semester, including the self-assessments at the end of each chapter. Many college programs use portfolio assessment for a variety of courses. Even if your college does not use this form of assessment, you can use a portfolio to reflect on your progress in writing and to determine what you need to concentrate on in your future writing classes.

The difference between a simple folder and a portfolio is that you and your instructor select pieces for the portfolio that show your development in this course as a writer. You will have copies of all your drafts and will have the reflection pieces from the self-assessment activities at the end of each chapter. These reflections will lead you to recognize your strengths and weaknesses and enable you to set goals for improvement. Finally, a complete portfolio would contain a reflection statement, written at the end of the semester, that summarizes what you have learned about your writing.

Writing Assignment 2

Using the three-step process for writing an academic paragraph (Gathering Information; Focusing and Organizing; and Writing, Editing, and Revising), write a paragraph of about 125 words analyzing the painting **Frida on the Border of Mexico and the United States.** *The main idea of the paragraph should report the main idea of the artist in this painting. Support this main idea by describing details from the painting and explaining how these details support the main idea.*

Frida on the Border of Mexico and the United States by Frida Kahlo, 1932. Mr. and Mrs. Manuel Reyero at New York.

▷ Gathering Information

EXERCISE **41** **Discussing with your classmates**

What do you know about Mexico and the United States? List information on the board.

EXERCISE 42   Learning more about Frida Kahlo

Do some research to learn more about Frida Kahlo.

Visit the College Writing 2 website for this textbook at http://esl.college.hmco.com/students for a listing of links that discuss Frida Kahlo and her art, or type in the keywords Frida Kahlo *in a search engine.*

OR

Go the library and look up Frida Kahlo *in a reference book.*

Take notes on one of the forms that follow:

Site Name: _____

URL: _____

Date visited: _____

New or interesting information:

Title: _____

Author/Publisher: _____

Date of Publication: _____

New or interesting information:

Report back to the class at least two new or interesting facts that you found.

EXERCISE 43 Freewriting

Spend five minutes writing about Frida Kahlo, her art, and the relationship between Mexico and the United States. Write any ideas that come to you. Don't worry about spelling, punctuation, organization, or grammar. Just write, and don't stop for five minutes!

EXERCISE 44 Developing vocabulary

Choose one sentence from your freewriting to share with the class.

Write the sentence on the board.

As a class, discuss the ideas and the vocabulary in the students' sentences.

Take notes on any vocabulary that you think you might find useful in writing your paragraph.

▷ Focusing and Organizing

EXERCISE 45 Developing ideas

Before you fill in the chart on page 37, answer the following questions with a partner. If you have problems with vocabulary words, use a dictionary or ask your instructor. After you have answered all the questions, you will be able to fill in the chart.

1. What are the objects in the painting?

2. What types of objects are on the Mexican side?

3. What types of objects are on the U.S. side?

4. What is Frida Kahlo holding? Why?

5. Is Frida Kahlo facing Mexico or the United States? Why?

6. What adjectives could describe the condition of the Mexican landscape?

7. What adjectives could describe the condition of the U.S. landscape?

8. What things cross the border? What do you think Frida Kahlo meant by painting these?

EXERCISE 46 Completing a chart

Fill in the chart with details from the picture and what you think the artist meant by these details.

Major details	Specific details	Adjectives that describe the condition of the objects	Why did the artist include these details? What do they mean?
Mexico (Objects)			
The United States (Objects)			
The Border (What is on the border?) (What crosses the border?)			

Because you cannot ask Frida Kahlo why she painted these details the way she did, you must make *inferences*, which are logical conclusions from the facts that you see. The details in the paintings are facts; the inferences that you make are opinions. Different students may have different opinions, but each opinion may be reasonable, as long as the student can explain it.

▽ Focusing and Organizing

EXERCISE 47   Developing the main idea

Compare your chart with a partner's.

Add details or inferences if you wish. Discuss what you think is the artist's main message in this painting.

Write a "working" topic sentence. (You may decide to change this sentence as you develop your paragraph.)

_____

_____

EXERCISE 48   Making an outline

On a separate sheet of paper, construct an outline for your paragraph.

Write down your working topic sentence from Exercise 47 above.

Decide which major details from the chart on page 37 to include in your paragraph.

Add specific details from the painting and your explanation of why these details support the main message of the artist.

Do not include any points or details that are not directly related to the main idea in your topic sentence.

EXERCISE 49   **Revising your topic sentence**

Reread the assignment for this paragraph (p. 34). Review your outline, and improve your topic sentence if necessary. Writing is a thinking process, so your ideas may develop or change as you continue to think about this assignment and as you write. Your topic sentence must include the main, overall idea for the paragraph. It should express what you believe the artist is saying in this painting.

EXERCISE 50   **Sharing your topic sentence**

Share your topic sentence with the class. Do some students express different ideas?

▷ Writing, Editing, and Revising

EXERCISE 51   **Writing your first draft**

Write the first draft of your paragraph. Be sure to indent the first line and to write from margin to margin. Use your outline to construct your paragraph. Begin with your topic sentence, and add sentences that give major details and specific supporting details. When you are finished with your supporting sentences, write a concluding sentence.

This is only your first draft, so you will have several opportunities to improve it. However, you should try to avoid errors that you made in the previous paragraph. Do not regard your instructor as your editor who will improve your paragraph by making corrections. She or he will not be with you after the end of the semester. You will need to know how to write correctly on your own. Once an error has been pointed out to you, it becomes your responsibility to eliminate it from your writing.

If you are not writing your paragraphs on a computer, you should be. Not only is it easier for your peer readers and your instructor but it is easier for you in the long run. When you need to revise and rewrite your paragraph, you can more easily and more quickly do that on a computer than by using paper and pencil.

EXERCISE 52   **Editing your paragraph**

Review your paragraph.

Underline each verb, and circle each subject.

Fill in the chart to make sure each verb is written in the correct tense.

Verb	Tense	Why did you choose this tense?

Make sure you have begun every sentence with a CAPITAL letter and have ended every sentence with a period.

Make sure each adjective is in front of its noun and each adjective clause is immediately after its noun.

Run the spell checker on the computer, or check your spelling with a dictionary.

Rewrite your paragraph.

EXERCISE 53   **Reviewing a classmate's paragraph**

Exchange your textbook and your paragraph with another student. Use the form below in your partner's textbook to review your partner's paragraph. Read the paragraph to see if the content is clear. Add any comments that you think would help the student improve the paragraph.

Peer Reader's Name: _____

Is the paragraph properly formatted?   Yes / No

Write down the controlling idea from the topic sentence.

_____

How many major points does the writer include in the paragraph?

_____

Does the paragraph have a concluding sentence?   Yes / No

Do all the sentences begin with a capital letter and
end with a period?   Yes / No

Do all the clauses have a subject and a verb?   Yes / No

Write down two subject-verb combinations. _____

Write down two adjectives from the paragraph. _____

Write down one adjective clause from the paragraph.

_____

Is the information clear to you?   Yes / No

Comments? _____

EXERCISE 54 Revising your paragraph

Reread the directions for this assignment (p. 34).

Reread the draft of your paragraph.

Consider the comments made by your partner.

> ▶ Was your writing clear?
> ▶ Was it organized?
> ▶ What changes can you make to improve your paragraph?

Think of your review of your partner's paragraph.

> ▶ What good features could you apply to your own paragraph?
> ▶ What errors did your partner make?
> ▶ Did you also make them?
> ▶ Did you learn anything from reviewing your partner's paragraph that could help improve your paragraph?

What other improvements can you make?

> ▶ Do you want to add more specific details?
> ▶ Have you used adjectives and adjective clauses to fully describe the picture?
> ▶ Do you want to change the order of the sentences or combine some sentences?

Rewrite your paragraph, and submit your paragraph to your instructor.

EXERCISE 55 Rewriting your paragraph

When you receive your paragraph back from your instructor, rewrite it as necessary. Place your drafts and your final paragraph in your folder.

SPOTLIGHT ON WRITING SKILLS

Editing Cards

You have now received feedback on your paragraph from a student and from your instructor. If they have noted errors that you made in this paragraph, eliminating those errors in future paragraphs now becomes your responsibility. If you do something incorrectly because you did not know the correct way to do it, that is understandable. If on the first day of this semester you handed in a paragraph without an indented first line, that was OK since you had not yet been taught to indent. However, now you have been taught the importance of indenting every paragraph, so it is no longer acceptable to make this mistake. Similarly, if a peer or your instructor pointed out an error in your writing (e.g., leaving the *-ed* ending off past tense verbs), you are now responsible for not making that particular mistake again.

One way to help yourself eliminate errors from your writing is to create an *editing card*. Write your name on an index card. Look over the review box that your classmate filled out for this paragraph and any notations that your instructor made on the draft. Write down on the index card the types of errors that were found in the draft—for example, *"left off verb endings," "forgot subjects in front of is and are," "didn't put a period at the end of every sentence," "unclear topic sentence."* For each writing assignment in this book, refer to this editing card when you are revising and editing your work. Then do not repeat mistakes you have made before.

During this semester, you might need to make new editing cards. This is actually a good sign since it would show that you are not making the same types of errors over and over again. Rather you are gaining control over your writing and eliminating errors that you have been making. At the same time, as your writing increases in complexity, you will naturally make new errors. Remember, the first time you make an error is not a problem. It is the repetition of errors that is a problem.

When you hand in your next paragraph, you will hand in this index card, too, so that your instructor can see how well you are editing.

▷ Additional Topics for More Practice and Assessment

Additional Writing Assignments

Choose one of the following writing tasks, and write one paragraph of about 125 words. Follow the process for writing that you have been practicing in this chapter (Gathering Information; Focusing and Organizing Ideas; and Writing, Editing, and Revising).

> Throughout the world and throughout history, political leaders have been depicted in statues and paintings, on coins and stamps. Choose one of these objects, and describe how the leader was portrayed.

> Visit an art gallery, and write a paragraph describing one of the pieces of artwork.

> Visit an art gallery online. Go to the College Writing 2 website for this textbook, http://esl.college.hmco.com/students, and click on the appropriate link. Choose a piece of art, and write a descriptive paragraph. If possible, attach a picture of the artwork to your paragraph.

Chapter 1 Self-Assessment

Do the following activities on a separate sheet of paper, and put the sheet into your folder.

Go back to page 3, and check whether you have accomplished the chapter's objectives. List the objectives you think you have accomplished in one column under the heading "Success." List the objectives you still need to practice in another column under the heading "Practice."

Write the three steps in writing an academic paragraph on the left side of a sheet of paper. Next to each step, write down your evaluation of your understanding of the step. Choose one of these comments: "I am confident I can do this," "I think I still need practice," I do not yet understand this step."

Answer the following questions:

1. In your opinion, what are the positive points of using an outline?
2. In your opinion, what are some negative points of using an outline?
3. Which was more challenging for you: listing the details from a painting or interpreting why the artist chose these details? Why?
4. What is the function of a topic sentence in a paragraph?
5. What are some of the functions of a concluding sentence?

Answer the following questions:

1. What makes an adjective clause a clause and not just an adjective?
2. Where are adjectives located in a sentence? What do they do?
3. Where are adjective clauses located in a sentence? What do they do?
4. What words are used to introduce adjective clauses?

Combine the information in these sentences into one sentence. Use adjectives and adjective clauses:

The painting is famous.
The painting is on exhibit in the art gallery.
The painting was done by Frida Kahlo.
The art gallery is privately owned.

Write two questions that you want to ask your instructor about the material or activities in this chapter.

WEB POWER

You will find additional exercises related to the content in this chapter at http://esl.college.hmco.com/students.

2

Organizing Information

Some psychologists believe that people's birth order in their families (e.g., oldest, youngest, or only child) affects their adult personalities. *First-born children are more responsible than youngest children. Middle children are peacemakers. Only children like to work alone rather than in groups.* What effect do you think your birth order has had on your personality?

Chapter Objectives

In this chapter, you will write at least two paragraphs in which you have to organize information to support a controlling idea. While completing these paragraphs, you will:	I have learned this well.	I need to work on this.
Distinguish general points from specific details		
Construct a concept map		
Construct a Venn diagram		
Put information in logical order in a paragraph		
Administer a survey		
Work effectively in a group		
Recognize signal words		
Use conjunctions appropriately		
Use transition words appropriately		
Use *has* and *have* correctly		

Review

PARAGRAPH ORGANIZATION

In Chapter 1, you wrote academic paragraphs. Each paragraph contained a topic sentence with a controlling idea, supporting information, and a concluding sentence. All academic paragraphs should contain this information.

The artwork in Chapter 1 was visual, so you could see the major details. In this chapter, you will be describing a personality, something that is not visible. Therefore, the more abstract term *major supporting points* will be used instead of *major supporting details*.

EXERCISE 1 Reviewing paragraph organization

Read Student Sample 1, and answer the questions that follow.

Student Sample 1

Topic Sentence —→

Major Supporting
Points with
Specific
Supporting
Details

Concluding
Sentence —→

My position as the firstborn child has helped me in many ways. **First of all**, I have always pushed myself in order to get better jobs. I am a perfectionistic, self-motivated, and responsible person. **Also**, this birth order has helped me in my daily work because I like to achieve goals. **On the other hand**, my brother is a little lazy and idealistic. He thinks that while he is studying, he will be okay. He has never worked because he has been studying for many years. I will never be like him because I am the oldest and have learned to accept challenges.

1. What is the controlling idea in the topic sentence?

   _____

2. How many major supporting points are there? _____

3. In the concluding sentence, what term does the student use that has

   the same meaning as "the firstborn child"? _____

EXERCISE **2** **Distinguishing general from specific**

With a partner, read Student Sample 2, and answer the questions that follow.

Student Sample 2

Topic Sentence
(most general)

Major Point #1
(more specific)

Specific Support
for #1
(detailed example)

Major Point #2
(more specific)

Specific Support
for #2
(detailed example)

Concluding
Sentence
(most general)

My younger brothers, who are twins, were born only fifteen minutes apart from each other, but they are very different in character. The oldest one, who is responsible and neat, does things to make other people happy and loves to cheer people up. Overall, he is a very caring person. For example, when I, the older sister, tell him to clean the house and wash the dishes, he does it so that he does not disappoint me. However, his twin is an irresponsible person who does things simply because he feels like it. In addition, he does not respect anyone who does not respect him. For example, when I get angry about some other things while at the same time talking to him, he thinks I am being disrespectful to him, so he gets mad and starts to shout at me. My twin brothers are very different people.

1. What is the controlling idea of this paragraph? _____

   _____

2. Which is more specific (narrower in meaning): the topic sentence or a

   major point? _____

3. Which is the most specific part of an academic paragraph: the topic

   sentence, a major point, a specific detail, or the concluding sentence?

   _____

4. How could the concluding sentence be revised so that the word

   different is not repeated? _____

Writing Assignment 1

In this assignment, you will write a paragraph of approximately 125 words that describes the personality of a close friend or relative. You will follow the steps of the writing process along with Lizbet, who has chosen to write about her cousin Jasmine.

▷ Gathering Information

Lizbet spent five minutes freewriting about her cousin, Jasmine.

EXERCISE 3 Freewriting

Freewrite for five minutes about the family member or close friend you choose to describe. Write as much as you can, without stopping. Do not worry about making mistakes. Instead, put all your ideas on paper.

▷ Focusing and Organizing

SPOTLIGHT ON WRITING SKILLS

Concept Maps

In Chapter 1, you used an outline format to organize your information before writing. Now, you will use a concept map to organize information before you write this paragraph. In a concept map, the main idea is written in the center, and the major points with their supporting details are grouped around the main idea.

EXERCISE 4 Constructing a concept map

Lizbet used the ideas in her freewriting to construct a concept map.

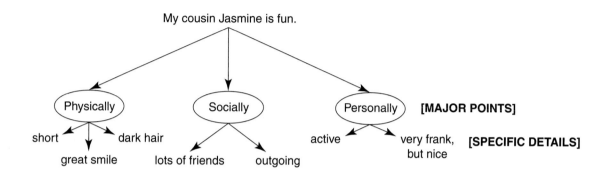

My cousin Jasmine is fun.

Physically   Socially   Personally   **[MAJOR POINTS]**

short   dark hair   active   very frank,   **[SPECIFIC DETAILS]**
                                                    but nice
great smile   lots of friends   outgoing

EXERCISE 5 Creating a concept map

In the space below, construct a concept map like Lizbet's to describe the personality of your friend or relative. Use ideas from your freewriting to complete the organizer. Remember: Your major points and specific details might be different from Lizbet's.

EXERCISE 6   **Focusing your concept map**

> Lizbet reread the assignment (to describe the personality of a friend
> or relative) and reviewed her concept map. She decided that her main
> idea would be her cousin's friendliness, so she changed her controlling
> idea. Then she crossed out the information that was not related to this
> controlling idea. For example, Jasmine is the oldest child in her family.
> She is short and has dark hair, and she is also active, but none of these
> facts are related to a description of her personality.

*Reread the assignment, and review your concept map. Then decide what the
main idea about your family member or close friend should be. Revise your
controlling idea if necessary. Cross out any information in your concept
map that does not relate to the main idea you have selected. An example is
shown below. If you need help, consult a classmate or your instructor.
Redraw your concept map in the space below.*

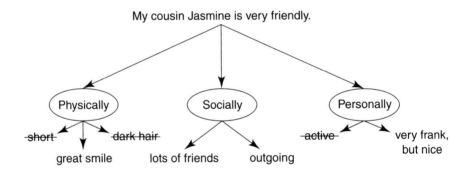

EXERCISE 7 Adding details to your concept map

> Lizbet added more specific details to the major points about Jasmine's friendliness. She added specific physical details that showed Jasmine's friendliness, specific social examples of friendliness, and specific personal information that showed her friendliness.

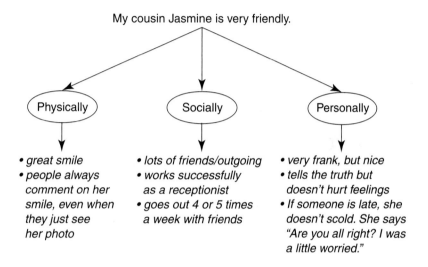

My cousin Jasmine is very friendly.

Physically
- *great smile*
- *people always comment on her smile, even when they just see her photo*

Socially
- *lots of friends/outgoing*
- *works successfully as a receptionist*
- *goes out 4 or 5 times a week with friends*

Personally
- *very frank, but nice*
- *tells the truth but doesn't hurt feelings*
- *If someone is late, she doesn't scold. She says "Are you all right? I was a little worried."*

Add details and examples to your graphic organizer about the person you are describing. Think of details that will interest your reader and support your main idea.

EXERCISE 8 Filling in an outline

> Lizbet used the information that she had gathered and organized to write a first draft of her paragraph.

Topic Sentence (most general) ———————→

Major Point #1 "outgoing"
(more specific)
Specific Support for #1 (most specific)

Major Point #2 "lots of friends"
(more specific)
Specific Support for #2 (most specific)

Major Point #3 "great smile"
(more specific)
Specific Support for #3 (most specific)

Major Point #4 "tells the truth" (more specific)
Specific Support for #4 (most specific)

Concluding Sentence

> My cousin Jasmine is an open and friendly person who is liked by others. She is successful in her job as a receptionist because she is outgoing. She welcomes clients and answers the phone warmly. Jasmine has lots of friends and she goes out four or five times a week. Her friends say that they like Jasmine because she has such a great smile. People always comment on it, even when they just see her photo. Another reason she is so popular is that she always tells the truth, but she does it nicely. For example, if a friend arrives very late, she does not scold the friend. Instead, she says, "Are you all right? I was a little worried." For all these reasons, Jasmine is one of the friendliest persons I have ever known.

Complete the outline with information from Lizbet's paragraph:

TOPIC SENTENCE _____

_____

Major Point #1 _____

Specific Detail to support Major Point #1 _____

Major Point #2 _____

Specific Detail to support Major Point #2 _____

Major Point #3 _____

Specific Detail to support Major Point #3 _____

Major Point #4 _____

Specific Detail to support Major Point #4 _____

EXERCISE 9 Thinking about your preferences

Visually, a concept map looks different from an outline, but mentally the organization of the information is the same. Answer these questions about your preferences.

1. Do you prefer to use a concept map or an outline? _____

2. What do you think is the reason for your preference? _____

_____

_____

_____

_____

▷ Writing, Editing, and Revising

EXERCISE 10 Writing your first draft

Reread Writing Assignment 1 (p. 50). Then use the information you have gathered, focused, and organized to write a rough (first) draft of your paragraph. Use the checklist to indicate what steps you have completed.

_____ 1. Indent the first sentence of the paragraph.

_____ 2. Leave margins on both the left and right sides of the page.

_____ 3. Begin with your topic sentence.

_____ 4. Write the major points and supporting ideas in complete sentences in your paragraph draft.

_____ 5. End with a concluding sentence that rephrases the topic sentence.

EXERCISE 11 **Checking your writing**

Underline each verb. Circle each subject. Make sure every clause has a subject and a verb.

Review every verb, and make sure you have used the correct tense.

Make sure you have begun every sentence with a CAPITAL letter and have ended every sentence with a period.

Check to make sure you have placed each adjective in front of the noun and each adjective clause directly after the noun.

Run the spell checker on your computer. If you are still not sure of the correct spelling of a word, use a dictionary.

Did you make any errors that you listed on your editing card in Chapter 1? If so, correct those errors.

Rewrite your paragraph if necessary.

SPOTLIGHT ON WRITING SKILLS

Peer Response

Reviewing your own writing is difficult. First, because you know what you intended to write, the meaning of your text is clear to you. It is frequently surprising to students that their writing is not clear to other readers. **The first goal of peer response is to help students see if their writing is communicating their ideas clearly to readers.** Do not take offense if another student does not understand your ideas. Focus on clarifying your writing.

A second <u>and even more important goal</u> is to help writers learn to self-edit, to identify language errors in their own writing. Because writers do not make errors deliberately, their writing seems correct when they read it to themselves. Errors are easier to see in someone else's writing, especially if you are reading it for the first time. Therefore, practice in checking other students' work for the accuracy of grammar, spelling, and punctuation is a first step in learning to edit your own work. Checking each verb ending or every period will give you experience in editing that you will be able to transfer to your own writing.

EXERCISE 12 Doing a peer response

Exchange your paragraph with your partner. Use Peer Response Form 2-1 in the appendix (p. 200) to respond to your partner's paragraph.

Return the paragraph and the peer response sheet to your partner.

Discuss the comments you and your partner made, and answer any questions your partner has.

Thank your partner for her or his assistance.

EXERCISE 13 Revising your writing

Reread the assignment. Then reread the draft of your paragraph.

Consider the comments made by your partner. What changes can you make to improve your paragraph?

Consider what you saw in your partner's paragraph. What did you like or dislike?

> ► Do you want to add more specific details?
> ► Do you want to change the order of the sentences or combine some sentences?
> ► Have you used adjectives and adjective clauses to fully describe the person's personality?
> ► What other improvements can you make?

Rewrite your paragraph.

Submit your paragraph to your instructor. Attach your editing card and the peer response sheet that your partner completed.

EXERCISE 14 Doing a final rewrite

When you receive your paragraph back from your instructor, revise and then rewrite your paragraph. Be sure to put your final copy and all your drafts into your folder.

EXERCISE 15 Updating your editing card

Add to your editing card if you made new errors.

EXERCISE 16 **Responding to feedback**

Complete the following survey:

1. When your instructor returned your paragraph, what did you look at

   first _____

   second _____

   third _____?

2. After your instructor returned your paragraph, how did you feel

   when you first looked at your paragraph? _____

   _____

3. When you looked at the marks and comments of your instructor, did

   you understand them? _____

4. What marks or comments did you find difficult to understand?

   _____

   _____

   _____

5. Are you able to correct your errors? _____

   If not, will you contact your instructor? _____

6. Do you agree with all the marks and comments? _____

   If yes, are you able to make appropriate changes to your paragraph?

   _____

   If no, what will you do? (Check the following action that you really
   will take.)

   _____ ignore the mark or comment

   _____ follow your instructor's advice

   _____ consult with your instructor

EXERCISE 17 Evaluating feedback

What marks and comments of your instructor did you find most helpful? Write a note to yourself answering this question. Share your note with your instructor if you wish.

SPOTLIGHT ON WRITING SKILLS

Group Work

In this chapter, you will be working in small, preferably three-person groups in which each member of the group will perform a specific task. For example, one student might be responsible for reading a set of questions aloud to the other students while a second student answers the questions. Finally, the third student might be responsible for writing the answers down on a piece of paper. Frequently, students will take turns performing different roles. While working together, you will develop skills that will help you individually in the writing process. In addition, you will be orally practicing your English language skills. An added bonus is that your group members will be immediately available to answer questions and to help you if you are confused.

Learning to effectively work in a group is not only an academic skill but an excellent skill for almost all future careers. The U. S. Department of Labor has published a report from the Secretary's Commission on Achieving Necessary Skills (SCANS) that outlines necessary skills that people need to succeed in the work world. One of those necessary skills is the ability to participate as a member of a team. Learning to work productively, efficiently and effectively, as a member of a group in your writing class will provide an excellent opportunity for you to develop this workplace skill.

Writing Assignment 2

This is a collaborative writing activity. You will work with other students in a small group to gather information about the subject of birth order by administering a survey to people not in your class. Then, in a group, you will focus and organize your information and write a paragraph that reports the results of the survey.

▷ Gathering Information

EXERCISE 18 Giving your opinion

Tell a partner your answers to the following questions:

1. Do the only children in families grow up to be self-centered or independent?
2. Do children in large families learn how to get along with people more easily than children in small families?
3. Are the oldest children in a family usually given more responsibilities than younger children?
4. Do middle children feel ignored? Does this affect their adult personalities?

WEB POWER

Visit the website for this text at
http://esl.college.hmco.com/students for a listing of websites that discuss birth order, or type in the keywords *birth order* and *personalities* in a search engine.

A. Visit two sites and take notes about what you find.
B. Complete a birth order survey at one of the sites. Follow the directions at the end of the survey to discover your results. In your opinion, did the results identify your birth order characteristics correctly?
C. Make a list of the personality characteristics associated with the results of the survey.

EXERCISE 19 Discussing with your classmates

On the board, list the personality characteristics related to different birth orders. Do most students agree with the descriptions? What is the source of the disagreements?

EXERCISE 20 Reviewing the survey form

This survey is designed to see if men and women have different views on the personalities of only children. In your small groups, review the survey. Discuss any questions that you find confusing.

---

1. NAME: _____ GENDER: M   F

2. Do you think an only child is usually lonely?   Yes   No

3. Do you think an only child is usually   Yes   No
   successful as an adult?

4. Which words do you think describe only children when they
   are young?

Intelligent	Lonely	Spoiled	Funny
Friendly	Passive	Outgoing	Active
Happy	No different from other children		

5. Which words do you think describe only children when they
   are adults?

Intelligent	Lonely	Bossy	Humorous
Competitive	Creative	Sarcastic	Worried
No different from other adults			

6. What comments do you have about birth order? _____

   _____

7. Your birth order in your family:

   Only   Oldest   Middle   Youngest   Twin

EXERCISE 21   Developing vocabulary

One student in the group should make a list of the adjectives from questions 4 and 5 and ask the other members of the group the meaning of each adjective.

Another student should be responsible for looking up the unknown adjectives from question 4.

The third student should be responsible for looking up the unknown adjectives from question 5.

EXERCISE 22   Setting up the survey

Each group member will give the survey to six people who are not in your class. Survey your friends, coworkers, and family members. Maybe you and your group will decide that you want to select only people in a certain age group. Perhaps you will decide that you want to ask people of different cultural backgrounds to respond to the survey.

Fill in the blanks:

WHERE WE WILL FIND PEOPLE TO SURVEY: _____

_____

_____

TYPES OF PEOPLE WE WILL SURVEY: _____

_____

_____

DEADLINE FOR COMPLETING SURVEY: _____

_____

_____

EXERCISE 23 Completing the survey

Each member of the group should complete the checklist below as he or she completes each activity.

_____ Make six copies of the survey. (There is a copy of the survey on p. 61.)

_____ Give a copy of the survey to six people (preferably three men and three women) who agree to complete it. Explain the purpose of the survey to each (to discover the attitude of survey respondents toward "only children").

_____ Tell each person how to return the survey, or collect the survey immediately.

_____ Answer any questions the people have.

_____ Thank each person for her or his participation.

_____ Bring the completed survey forms to class.

▷ Focusing and Organizing

EXERCISE 24 Organizing data

After each group member has collected six surveys, combine the data from all the surveys onto the data collection sheet (pp. 64–65).

One student adds up the numbers from the surveys.

One student records all the information onto the charts.

One student checks the final results.

Data collection sheet

	Men		Women	
Only child	**# Yes**	**# No**	**# Yes**	**# No**
Lonely as child				
Successful as adult				

	Men	Women
Only child when young	**Mark each adjective which a majority (50%+) chose.**	
Intelligent		
Lonely		
Spoiled		
Funny		
Friendly		
Passive		
Outgoing		
Active		
Happy		
No different		

Only child as adult	Men	Women
	Mark each adjective which a majority (50%+) chose.	
Intelligent		
Lonely		
Bossy		
Humorous		
Competitive		
Creative		
Sarcastic		
Worried		
No different		

Did you receive any interesting comments on the survey? If so, list them here.

_____

_____

Did you notice any interesting differences in answers of people of different birth orders? If so, list them here.

_____

_____

SPOTLIGHT ON WRITING SKILLS

Venn Diagrams

You have already used two types of graphic organizers: an outline and a concept map. Now you will use a Venn diagram. A Venn diagram uses overlapping circles to represent groups of ideas or objects. Each circle part that does not overlap contains information about only one of the groups. The section where the circles overlap contains information common to all of the groups.

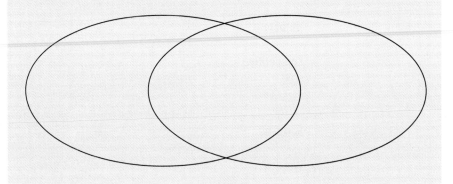

EXERCISE 25   Using a Venn diagram

Now, organize your information from both the men and the women. Put the ideas that a majority (50+ percent) of men chose into one circle and the ideas from a majority of women into the other circle. Any information that is common to both groups should be placed in the center, where both circles overlap.

- ► *One student announces the information.*
- ► *One student writes the information on the diagram.*
- ► *One student checks the completed diagram for accuracy.*

How only children are viewed:

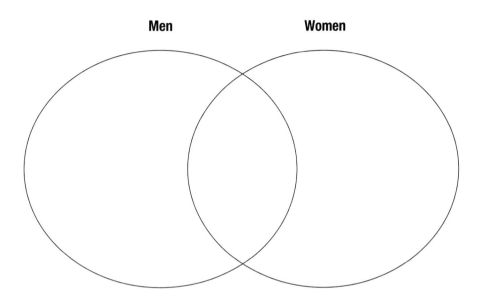

EXERCISE 26 Focusing the information

With your group, review the Venn diagram and choose the two to four ideas that are most important. Eliminate the least chosen adjectives. For example, if an adjective was chosen by only five of nine women but another adjective was chosen by nine of nine women, the first adjective is not as well supported. You could eliminate it if you wanted.

EXERCISE 27 **Adding interesting details**

Review the comments made by your respondents. With your group, discuss which respondents' comments you should add to your report. With your group, decide whether or not there are any interesting differences between respondents of different genders or different birth orders. Perhaps some survey takers had interesting comments. Attach these details to your diagram, as illustrated in the picture.

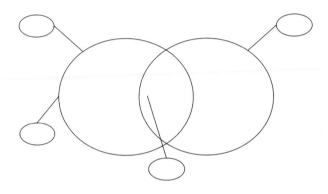

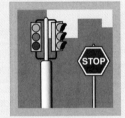

SPOTLIGHT ON WRITING SKILLS

Signal Words

Reading can be compared to driving a car. Drivers who are traveling on familiar streets do not get lost even if a street sign is missing. They know the way to their destinations and can smoothly travel along streets without needing directions.

However, even excellent drivers can have trouble reaching a destination in an unfamiliar city if they lack directions or if the streets are unmarked. When you write, you are like an experienced driver. You know how your sentences relate to one another and to your topic sentence. You know when you shift from one major point to another, and you know when you reach your concluding sentence. However, your readers are like first-time visitors. Even excellent readers can have trouble figuring out the point of a paragraph if there are no signals to guide them through the unfamiliar text. Your readers need clear directions, which you can give them by using **signal words**, such as *but, also, for example,* and *so.*

POWER GRAMMAR

Coordinating Conjunctions

One way to signal the flow of ideas is by using <u>coordinating conjunctions</u>.

These small words—*and*, *but*, *so*, *or*, and a few others—are directional "signs" for readers.

A first-born child is usually responsible, **but** some older children rebel against their families' demands. (The word *but* signals that the idea in the second clause is opposite the first.)

Many only children learn to speak at a very young age, **and** their language development as adults is often remarkable.

(The word *and* signals that the second clause is additional information.)

Identical twins are easily mistaken for one another, **so** parents sometimes use color-coded clothing or bracelets to identify the children.

(The word *so* signals that the use of color-coded clothing is the result of the parents' fear of mistaking the children.)

A comma comes before each coordinating conjunction that joins two independent clauses.

<u>I am the oldest child in my family</u>, **and** <u>I have one younger brother</u>.

If the coordinating conjunction joins two nouns or two verbs or two phrases or two adjectives, no comma is used.

Whether a youngest child is <u>loving</u> **or** <u>demanding</u> might depend on the type of attention the child receives.

He thinks I am being disrespectful to him, **so** he gets mad **and** starts to shout at me.

Refer to Appendix 2 (p. 200) for a complete listing of coordinating conjunctions and an easy way to remember which words are coordinating conjunctions.

EXERCISE 28   **Comprehending different conjunctions**

Explain why the underlined coordinating conjunctions were used to join the following pairs of clauses.

> **Example:** First-born children are rule-keepers, <u>and</u> they frequently make rules for the younger children in their families.

> AND shows the reader that the second independent clause <u>*is additional information*</u>.

1. The first-born child wants the last-born child to follow the rules, <u>but</u> the last-born child will not usually listen to the older sibling.

   BUT indicates that the next information _____

   _____.

2. Youngest children often do not feel responsible for the other people in their families, <u>so</u> they sometimes act irresponsibly.

   SO signals the reader that the next independent clause _____

   _____.

EXERCISE 29   **Locating the connected words**

Read the following student sample. The coordinating conjunctions are in bold.

> I am the oldest in my family, **and** I have one younger brother. My younger brother is only one year **and** ten months younger, **but** our characters are very different. I am flexible, a peacemaker, **but** my brother is uncompromising. I don't like to argue, **but** my brother likes to argue all the time. My parents frequently leave me in charge of the house, **so** often I have to negotiate with my brother to keep peace. My character might depend on my "seniority," **or** my brother's character might depend on his "juniority"; I am not sure.

On the lines below, write the words joined by the coordinating conjunctions and list the relationships that the conjunctions indicate. The first one has been done for you.

1. I am the older brother in my family **and** I have one younger brother.

   Relationship: additional information

2. _____ **and** _____ (Hint: Is there a comma?)

   Relationship: _____

3. _____ **but** _____

   Relationship: _____

4. _____ **but** _____

   Relationship: _____

5. _____ **but** _____

   Relationship: _____

6. _____ **so** _____

   Relationship: _____

7. _____ **or** _____

   Relationship: _____

Write the rule for using or not using a comma with coordinating conjunctions.

_____

_____

_____

EXERCISE 30 **Working with coordinating conjunctions**

Join the following pairs of sentences with the word in parentheses ( ).
Be sure to use a comma before the coordinating conjunction.

1. A survey is a written list of statements or questions about a single topic.
   A group of people, called "respondents," are asked to read and respond to the survey.

   (and) [additional information]

   _____

   _____

   _____

2. Most people do not want to spend a lot of time filling out a survey.
   Surveys should be short and contain clear questions or statements and nontechnical vocabulary.

   (so) [information about a result]

   _____

   _____

   _____

3. Many surveys ask respondents to choose one answer from several possible answers.
   A few ask questions and expect respondents to write individual answers to those questions.

   (but) [contrasting information]

   _____

   _____

   _____

4. A survey might include multiple-choice questions.
   It could use True/False questions.

   (or) [choice]

   _____

   _____

   _____

▷ Writing, Editing, and Revising

EXERCISE 31 Developing a topic sentence

Writing Assignment 2 is to gather information about the subject of birth order by administering a survey to people not in your class and then write a paragraph that reports the results of the survey.

Discuss with your group the major idea from your survey results.

Write the major idea: _____

_____

Each person in your group should write a topic sentence (which should give the main idea from the survey). It should describe how the effect of this particular birth order (only child) on the development of adult personalities is viewed by men and women. The topic sentence must contain the overall idea, not the supporting information. Perhaps a coordinating conjunction would clearly show the relationship between the opinion of men and the opinion of women.

Because you are reporting the results of your survey, not just your own ideas, begin the sentence with a reference to the source of the information. For example, "According to our survey, men and women …".

Topic Sentence: _____

_____

_____

Share your topic sentence with the other members of your group. Discuss any improvements you could make. Decide on one topic sentence.

Write the group's topic sentence on an index card or a small piece of paper.

SPOTLIGHT ON WRITING SKILLS

Choose a Pattern of Organization

Reread Student Sample 2 (p. 49). Notice how the information is organized.

> ► The topic sentence, with the overall idea, is presented at the beginning. (The twins are very different in character.)
> ► Then information on one twin is given. (Major Point #1 with specific supporting details)
> ► The information on the second twin, who is very different from his brother, follows. (Major Point #2 with specific supporting details)
> ► Finally, the last sentence draws a conclusion.

This is one pattern of organization for information about two different items. You may choose to present all the information about one item and then all the information about the other item. If your survey showed different viewpoints from men and women, you could organize your paragraph with this pattern.

If your survey results showed no important differences between the viewpoints of men and women, then you could use the following pattern of organization.

> ► Begin with a topic sentence that explains that there was no important difference in the viewpoints of men and women on this topic.
> ► Then list several major supporting points. For each point, give some specific details from both men and women.
> ► Finally, write a concluding sentence.

EXERCISE 32 Deciding on a pattern of organization

With your group, decide how you will organize the information in your paragraph.

EXERCISE 33 Putting ideas in logical order

In your group, use the information from the survey that you have organized and focused to write sentences that support and explain your topic sentence (Exercise 29). Each sentence should be written on a separate index card or a small piece of paper. These cards will then be sorted into the pattern of organization that your group has chosen.

Put supporting information into sentence form:

- ► One student writes a sentence on a card.
- ► Another student reviews the sentence to see if the information is correct and if the sentence has been written correctly. He or she corrects the sentence if necessary.
- ► Students switch roles until several sentences have been written.

Put sentences into logical order:

- ► One student puts the cards into the pattern of organization that the group has chosen. The student may remove cards if the information does not support the controlling idea of the topic sentence.
- ► Another student checks the organization. If this student does not agree with the organization, then he or she should suggest changes. All members of the group should agree with the final pattern of organization.
- ► A third student should decide if the information is complete. If it is not complete, then the student should write a sentence that will fill any gaps in the paragraph or will add interesting details to the paragraph.

Save the cards in order. The card with the topic sentence should be first.

POWER GRAMMAR

Transition Words and Expressions

In academic paragraphs, writers use a variety of signal words to help readers understand connections between ideas. Coordinating conjunctions are one type of signal. Transition words and expressions are another.

Transition words and expressions are not frequently used in conversational speech, but they are frequently used in written English. Like coordinating conjunctions, these words serve as signals to the reader. They identify the relationship between the ideas in two sentences or even between ideas in two paragraphs.

... in many ways. **First of all**, ... (This shows the beginning of a list of ways.)

... I like to achieve goals. **On the other hand**, ... (Contrasting information will be introduced.)

He is a very caring person. **For example**, ...(A specific example showing how he cares will be next.)

... so that he does not disappoint me. **However**, ... (Contrasting information will be introduced.)

Unlike coordinating conjunctions, transition words may be punctuated in three ways. Independent clause [period]

A large family means a lot of work. **However**, the children can help with many of the jobs.

Transition word [comma] independent clause.

Independent clause [semicolon] **transition word** [comma] independent clause.

A large family means a lot of work; **however**, the children can help with many of the jobs.

Independent clause [period] Independent [comma] **transition word** [comma] clause. (You may see this punctuation in readings but will probably not use it in your writing at this level.)

A large family means a lot of at work. The children, **however**, can help with many of the jobs.

Refer to Appendix 1 (p. 198) for a listing of transition words and expressions.

EXERCISE 34 Combining sentences with transition words

Join the following pairs of sentences with the word in parentheses ( ).
Be sure to use a comma after the transition word(s). Join the sentences
a second time, but punctuate them differently.

1. Many surveys ask respondents to choose one answer from several
    possible answers.
    A few ask questions and expect respondents to write individual
    answers to those questions.   (However) [contrasting information]

    A. _____

    _____

    _____

    _____

    B. _____

    _____

    _____

    _____

2. Most people do not want to spend a lot of time filling out a survey.
    Surveys should be short and contain clear questions and nontechnical
    vocabulary.   (Therefore) [information about a result]

    A. _____

    _____

    _____

    _____

    B. _____

    _____

    _____

    _____

3. A survey is a written list of statements or questions about a single topic. A group of people, called "respondents," is asked to read and respond to the survey.   (Also) [additional information]

A. _____

_____

_____

B. _____

_____

_____

EXERCISE 35 **Understanding transition words**

Reread Student Sample 1 on page 48. The transition words and expressions are in bold. On the blank lines below, write the meaning(s) of the word(s). The first one is completed for you.

1. First of all, *lists the first reason why being the first-born is an*

advantage.

2. Also, _____

_____

3. On the other hand, _____

_____

EXERCISE 36 **Combining sentences with transition words**

Join the following pairs of sentences by using the words in parentheses ( ). Be sure to punctuate correctly.

1. (Therefore) Youngest children are usually creative. They frequently enjoy art and music.

_____

_____

_____

2. (In contrast) First-born children want to be perfect in everything.
   Last-born children are more relaxed and want to enjoy life.

   _____

   _____

   _____

3. (In fact) Only children are used to getting a lot of attention from
   adults. They frequently like to play with adults rather than other
   children.

   _____

   _____

   _____

EXERCISE 37 **Adding transition words**

*Using the cards from Exercise 33, suggest transition words that will clearly
show the logic of the paragraph's organization and help readers understand
the ideas expressed by the writers. Write the words on separate index cards
or pieces of paper, and put them in order with the sentences that the group
has already organized.*

EXERCISE 38 **Writing a concluding sentence**

*Go back to pages 48–49, and reread the concluding sentences in the
students' paragraphs. Decide what your paragraph's concluding sentence
will do:*

- ► Restate the main idea
- ► Ask for a response
- ► Evaluate the topic
- ► Make a suggestion
- ► State a prediction

*Write a concluding sentence on an index card, and put it last in the
group's pile.*

EXERCISE 39 **Writing your first draft**

Each student should write the group's paragraph on a sheet of paper.

SPOTLIGHT ON WRITING SKILLS

Ear Learners and the Verb *Have*

In spoken English, the verb *have* is frequently difficult to hear.

► Often, *have* is barely pronounced: "*I have completed the survey*" is spoken quickly and sounds like "*I'ff completed the survey.*" The distinction between *have* and *has* is very difficult to perceive because these words are often not clearly pronounced or are pronounced quickly in a contraction. "*The teacher **has** given some examples*" is sometimes spoken "*The teacher's given some examples.*" "*The students would **have** completed their paragraphs if they **had had** the time*" is sometimes pronounced "*The students would **of** completed their paragraphs if they'd **had** the time.*"

As a result, "ear" learners need to practice writing the correct form of the verb *have* to avoid making this common but confusing error.

One way to help you recognize how to write the correct verb form is to remember how the verb *have* is used. One reason that the verb *have* is difficult is that it is both a primary verb and a helping verb. In the sentence "*The students have a lot of information for their paragraph,*" *have* is a primary verb. It shows possession or ownership. In the sentence "*The students have distributed thirty surveys to people in the cafeteria,*" the verb *have* is a helping verb. The primary verb is *distribute*. When you are reading and you come across the verb *have*, look at how the verb is used.

Students also need to remember when to use *have* and when to use *has*. Again, be alert when you read. Notice the subject, which controls the spelling of the verb. If the subject is *I, you, we,* or *they,* the verb is *have*. If the subject is *he, she, it,* or refers to some other single person or thing, the verb is *has*.

EXERCISE 40 Hearing "Whaddya Say?"

What we hear is not always what we write!

Write the sentences you hear. Write out all the verbs.

1. _____
   _____
   _____

2. _____
   _____
   _____

3. _____
   _____
   _____

4. _____
   _____
   _____

5. _____
   _____
   _____

6. _____
   _____
   _____

EXERCISE 41 Checking your answers

Compare your sentences with a partner's. Do your sentences agree?

Underline all the verbs in your sentences.

EXERCISE 42 **Making a choice between *have* and *has***

Circle the correct verb. Write the subject on the line.

Example:

The concept of birth order ((has) / have) become a popular theory in recent years.

The subject is _concept_, which is singular.

1. Mr. and Mrs. Jimenez (has / have) three children who live at home.

   The oldest child (has, have) been paying rent for the past year.

   The subject is _____, which is plural.

   The subject is _____, which is singular.

2. Since their fourth child was born, Mr. and Mrs. Metz (has, have) not had time to see a movie.

   The subject is _____, which is plural.

3. Frequently, first-born children (has, have) the job of baby-sitting younger siblings [brothers and sisters].

   The subject is _____, which is plural.

4. If you (has, have) never known identical twins, you might be surprised at the behaviors that (has, have) been observed in studies of these twins.

   The subject is _____.

   The subject is _____, which is the pronoun in place of behaviors, which is plural.

Have always follows the subjects *you, I, they,* and *we.*

EXERCISE 43 Comparing your answers with a partner's

Compare your answers to Exercise 42 with the answers of a partner. If you disagree, explain why you answered as you did. If you cannot resolve the difference, ask your instructor.

EXERCISE 44 Finishing sentences with *have* and *has*

Finish the sentences.

How many siblings do you have? I _____.

How many siblings does the student next to you have? He or she

_____.

How many siblings does an only child have? An only child

_____ any siblings.

Irina and her brother Alex are responsible for the cooking and

cleaning in their home. They _____ a lot of responsibilities.

Mrs. Patel _____ four children and two cats, but she

_____ any dogs.

EXERCISE 45 **Locating the verb *have***

Read this student's paragraph, and circle each example of the verb have.

Student Sample 4

Being the second child in my family has affected me in many ways. My older brother is just one year older than me, and we have had a very close relationship. That is why I try to have close friendships. When we were kids, I always wanted to be like him and have exactly what he had. We used to be dressed like twins! I believe that is the reason why I am attracted to what my friends have, which gives me ambition to have the same things. On the other hand, I have a small brother who is seven years younger than me, and all his life I have wanted to protect him and give him everything he wants. That is why I am a giving person. Being the middle child made me a compromising person because I always tried to get my younger brother out from troubles and protect him from my older one.

EXERCISE 46 **Using *have* and *has* in a paragraph**

With your group, reread your paragraph about the survey and underline each have *or* has. *Circle the subject of each of these verbs. Mark each singular subject with an S and each plural subject with a P. Make sure that each S subject is followed by* has *and that each P subject is followed by* have.

EXERCISE 47 **Checking your writing**

Circle every subject, and underline every verb. Check every clause to be sure it has a subject and a verb.

Check every verb to be sure it has the correct tense.

Check that any coordinating conjunctions are punctuated properly.

Check that transition words will help your readers understand the logical connection between your ideas.

Run a computer spell checker on your writing. If you are still not sure of the correct spelling of a word, use a dictionary.

Review your editing cards to be sure you are not repeating errors.

Rewrite your paragraph if necessary.

EXERCISE 48 Doing a peer response

Exchange paragraphs with students from another group. Using Peer Response Form 2-2 (p. 201), review the new paragraph.

EXERCISE 49 Revising your paragraph

With your group, discuss the comments from the other students.

Revise your paragraph, using the comments given by your peer reviewers.

Discuss what you learned from doing the review of the other paragraphs. What other improvements can you make in your paragraph?

Rewrite your revised and edited paragraph. Put the names of all the group's members on the bottom of the paper.

Submit your paragraph to your instructor. Be sure to attach Peer Response Form 2-2 and your editing card.

EXERCISE 50 Updating your editing card

When your instructor returns your paragraph, note any new errors on your editing card.

EXERCISE 51 Rewriting your paragraph

If necessary, rewrite your paragraph. Place your revised paragraph and all drafts in your folder.

▷ Additional Topics for More Practice and Assessment

Additional Writing Assignments

Choose one of the following writing tasks, and write one paragraph of about 125 words. Follow the process for writing that you have been practicing in this chapter (Gathering Information; Focusing and Organizing Ideas; and Writing, Editing, and Revising).

A. Write a paragraph expressing your opinion on the effect of a particular birth order (oldest child, middle child, twin, …) on adult personalities. Support your opinion with information from the websites you have visited or from your own personal experience.

B. With a group, design a new survey that researches a different viewpoint on birth order. (Do different cultural groups have different views on birth order? Are first-born children always the most responsible? Does a big age gap between children make a big difference in their birth order characteristics?) Write a paragraph about your findings. Although you can work in a group to gather the information and organize it, you should write this paragraph independently.

C. Go to the Houghton Mifflin website for this textbook, http://esl.college.hmco.com/students, and report on the research on birth order done by one of the links.

D. Borrow a psychology book from the library or from a friend, and report on what it says about adult personalities and birth order.

Chapter 2 Self-Assessment

Do the following activities on a separate sheet of paper, and put the sheet into your folder.

A. Go back to page 47, and check whether you have accomplished the chapter's objectives. List the objectives you think you have accomplished in one column under the heading "Success." List the objectives you still need to practice in another column under the heading "Practice."

B. "Understanding the assignment is an important step not only in writing an academic paragraph but also in any college assignment." Do you agree or disagree with this statement? Why?

C. Answer the following questions.

1. Which step in the process of writing an academic paragraph is the most difficult for you? Why?
2. How many different types of writing do you do in your daily life outside college?
3. In what ways were the graphic organizers (outline, concept map, Venn diagram) useful to you? Would you use them again? Why or why not?
4. What suggestions do you have for helping other students learn differences between oral and written language forms?
5. What, in your opinion, are the most important points to remember for using *have* and *has* correctly?

D. Read an article in a magazine or a page from a textbook, and list the signal words (p. 68) you find. Why did the writer choose to use these specific words?

E. Write down two questions you want to ask your instructor about the material or activities in this chapter.

W E B   P O W E R

You will find additional exercises related to the content in this chapter at http://esl.college.hmco.com/students.

Reporting Information

One of the most frequent uses of academic writing is to report information obtained from research and reading. In this chapter you will research a career that interests you and report on the information that you learn from reviewing internet sources and interviewing a person employed in your chosen field.

Academic Writing Objectives

In this chapter, you will write at least two paragraphs in which you will report information from outside sources. While completing these paragraphs you will:	I have learned this well.	I need to work on this.
Write paragraphs that have clear controlling ideas and ample supporting information		
Take notes from reference material		
Use a chart to help organize information		
Conduct an interview and take clear notes		
Present information logically		
Use transition words appropriately		
Edit your paragraphs so that you are not repeating mistakes from previous paragraphs		
Cite research material correctly		
Identify people clearly and accurately		
Use verb tenses correctly		

Writing Assignment 1

Write a paragraph describing your chosen major or occupation. To complete this assignment, you will locate information in your college's career counseling center or on the Internet. You will follow the steps of Gathering Information; Focusing and Organizing; and Writing, Editing, and Revising to write a paragraph reporting the information. **(You will need to fill in the form on page 95 before you can write the paragraph.)**

▷ Gathering Information

EXERCISE 1 Reading an occupation information worksheet

Read the Occupation Information Worksheet that follows, which a student completed from information on the U.S. Department of Labor's website.

Source of Information—*Occupational Outlook Handbook 2002–2003*, published online by the U.S. Department of Labor, http://www.bls.gov/oco/, 1/31/03

(Whenever you present information in an academic assignment, you must cite [identify] the source of the information. Always be careful to write down all the identifying information you will need before you finish taking notes from the source. For the Department of Labor source, you must write down the title of the document, date of publication, the URL, and the date you retrieved the information.)

Occupation—**Airline Pilot**

Nature of work:

Major Point

Four-fifths of aircraft pilots work for airlines, others are commercial pilots—do things like cropdusting . . .
Usually 2 pilots = 1 plane. Captain is in charge
Takeoffs and landings are the hardest part
Very technical now, lots of instruments and computers!!!

Supporting Details

(Continued)

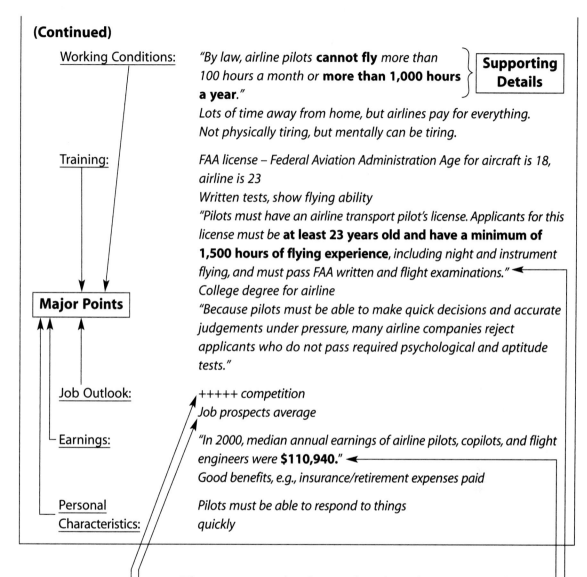

Working Conditions:

"By law, airline pilots **cannot fly** *more than 100 hours a month or* **more than 1,000 hours a year.***"* ⎫ **Supporting Details**

Lots of time away from home, but airlines pay for everything.
Not physically tiring, but mentally can be tiring.

Training:

FAA license – Federal Aviation Administration Age for aircraft is 18, airline is 23
Written tests, show flying ability
"Pilots must have an airline transport pilot's license. Applicants for this license must be **at least 23 years old and have a minimum of 1,500 hours of flying experience,** *including night and instrument flying, and must pass FAA written and flight examinations."*
College degree for airline
"Because pilots must be able to make quick decisions and accurate judgements under pressure, many airline companies reject applicants who do not pass required psychological and aptitude tests."

Major Points

Job Outlook:

+++++ competition
Job prospects average

Earnings:

"In 2000, median annual earnings of airline pilots, copilots, and flight engineers were **$110,940.***"*
Good benefits, e.g., insurance/retirement expenses paid

Personal Characteristics:

Pilots must be able to respond to things quickly

These are notes, taken by a student, from the *Occupational Outlook Handbook*. It is not all the information available from this source; the notes include important and interesting information.

▶ Notes are personal, so these notes have not been written formally. **Abbreviations and symbols** have been used; **phrases** are usually used instead of sentences; **important information** has been highlighted.

▶ Language taken exactly from the text is inside **quotation marks.** The quotation marks help you remember which of the notes are your own words and which are quoted from the source.

EXERCISE 2 **Reading a paragraph**

Read Student Sample 1, and notice the information from the worksheet (pp. 90–91).

Student Sample 1

According to the U.S. Department of Labor's (DOL), *online Occupational Outlook Handbook 2002–2003* (January 31, 2003), a career as an airline pilot requires intensive training but offers many personal and financial benefits. To qualify to be an airline pilot, a person must "have a minimum of 1,500 hours of flying experience, including night and instrument flying, and must pass FAA written and flight examinations." (DOL) Also, most airlines require a college degree. In addition, "because pilots must be able to make quick decisions and accurate judgments under pressure, many airline companies reject applicants who do not pass required psychological and aptitude tests." (DOL) Finally, pilots must continue training as long as they are flying. While becoming a pilot is difficult, being a pilot has many great benefits. First of all, pilots have very high earnings. In 2000, the average airline pilot earned over $110,000. (DOL) Second, most airlines offer good insurance and retirement benefits to pilots, and the airline pays for all expenses when the pilot is away from home. Finally, pilots cannot fly more than 1,000 hours a year (DOL), so pilots can have a lot of free time. A career as an airline pilot seems to be worth all the time and training it takes to become one.

References

Occupational Outlook Handbook 2002–2003
http://www.bls.gov/oco/1/31/03

SPOTLIGHT ON WRITING SKILLS

Using Citations

Whenever you present information or ideas that you did not know when you began to gather information about a topic, you must give credit to the source—the person(s) or institution(s) whose information or ideas you are using. If you use the exact words from the source, you must put these words in quotation marks. If you rephrase the information, you must still give credit to the source. For example, in Student Sample 1, the writer has identified (cited) the source in two ways:

1. immediately after the writer used the information in the paragraph, a short in-text citation; this in-text citation lets the readers know that the information came from a source.
2. at the end of the paragraph, a complete reference for the citation. **End-of-text citations** give the readers enough information to find the source themselves. List these complete citations under the heading "References."

Most academic writing assignments require you to find sources that support your ideas and opinions. Therefore, in most academic writing assignments, you must cite (identify) the source of the information. Writers include as much of the following information as is available:

► the title of the source
► the author (writer)
► the publisher
► the date of publication
► the page numbers where the direct quotations were taken

Your college library/writing center will have information on how to write citations. Many college library/writing centers offer online guidance on how to properly cite sources.

Locate your college's resources and report back to your class what you learned. If handouts are available, make sure you take copies.

Master Student Tip

▼ When taking notes, always be careful to write down all the identifying information that you will need to cite a source.

EXERCISE 3 **Comparing the notes and the paragraph**

Use the Occupation Information Worksheet (p. 95) and Student Sample 1 to complete the following questions:

Underline the information in the student's paragraph that comes directly from the student's notes.

Why did the student put only certain parts of the information in quotation marks?

_____

_____

Underline the details in the notes that the student left out of the paragraph.

Why do you think the student left out that information?

_____

_____

Circle the words the student used to connect the major points in the paragraph.

Are they effective?

_____

_____

EXERCISE 4 **Filling in the worksheet**

Choose an occupation that you are interested in, and use the Occupational Outlook Handbook *and/or other resources available in your college counseling center or library to fill in the Occupation Information Worksheet on page 95.*

AND/OR

Visit the website for this text at http://esl.college.hmco.com/students for a link to the Occupational Outlook Handbook *and a listing of other websites that offer information on occupations. Use the information to complete the Occupation Information Worksheet.*

Occupation Information Worksheet

Source of Information: _____

Occupation: _____

Nature of Work

Working Conditions

Training

Job Outlook

Earnings

Personal Characteristics

▷ Focusing and Organizing

EXERCISE 5   Developing a controlling idea

Use your notes to complete the following activities.

Review your notes, and decide what your main idea, opinion, or attitude is about the occupation you have chosen.

_____

_____

Explain to a partner why you decided on your main idea, opinion, or attitude about your chosen occupation.

EXERCISE 6   Choosing supporting information

The Occupation Information Worksheet is divided into <u>major points</u>. What you added to the form are the <u>supporting details</u>. Review this information.

Highlight the information you want to include in your paragraph.

Cross out any major point (and all the information in that section of the form) that you do not think is relevant or important. You cannot use a specific detail from a major point that you have eliminated.

Perhaps not all the specific details for a major point are interesting or informative. Cross out the details you choose not to include.

EXERCISE 7   Writing your topic sentence

Write your topic sentence. Begin with your information source—for example, "According to the Occupational Outlook Handbook," or "The College Placement Annual states that . . .," or "As stated on www.ajb.dni.us." In your topic sentence, include the career and the major idea, opinion, or attitude about it that you will focus on in your paragraph.

_____

_____

_____

Showing Logical Connections Between Ideas

How will you logically connect the major points in your paragraph? In other words, will you use a simple list, or will you explain how one point is more important than the others? Use transition words to indicate the logical connection between the major points in your paragraph.

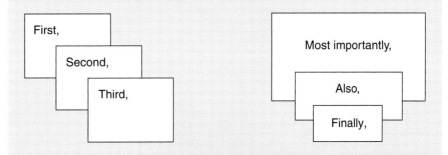

For example, *First ...*, *Second ...*, *Third ...* would indicate a simple list of points, whereas *Most importantly ...*, *Also ...*, *Finally ...* would indicate the decreasing importance of the points. (Remember the explanation on p. 68 about signals?)

EXERCISE 8   Using a chart as a graphic organizer

Use the chart on page 98 as a graphic organizer.

List the major points that you will include to explain, describe, clarify, or support this topic sentence. (These should be the headings from the Occupation Information Worksheet you filled out.)

On the lines to the left of the numbers in the chart, write the transition words you think you will use.

Review your notes to decide which specific details you will include with each major point. Add them to your chart. Be sure to put the specific details next to the corresponding major point.

Transition   Major Point

_____ 1.   _____

        Specific Details

        _____

        _____

        _____

Major Point

_____ 2.   _____

        Specific Details

        _____

        _____

        _____

Major Point

_____ 3.   _____

        Specific Details

        _____

        _____

        _____

▷ Writing, Editing, and Revising

EXERCISE 9 **Writing your first draft**

Reread Writing Assignment 1 (p. 90). Then use the information you have gathered, focused, and organized to write a first rough draft of your paragraph. Use the checklist to indicate the steps you complete.

1. _____ Indent the first sentence of the paragraph.

2. _____ Leave margins on both the left and right sides of the page.

3. _____ Write the topic sentence.

4. _____ Write the major points and supporting ideas in complete sentences.

5. _____ Use transition words to introduce major points.

6. _____ Look at Student Sample 1 on page 92, and follow the example for using citations.

   ► Use two direct quotations from the *Occupational Outlook Handbook* (or other source you used for your information).
   ► Use an in-text citation for each direct quotation.
   ► Use an end-of-text citation at the end of the paragraph. Remember to center the "References" heading.

7. _____ Look at Student Sample 1 on page 92 and the Power Grammar on page 106. Follow the examples for using reported speech for other information in your paragraph. Remember to use an in-text citation for any specific information in your paragraph.

8. _____ End your paragraph with a concluding sentence that rephrases the topic sentence or reflects the overall idea on the topic.

EXERCISE 10 Checking your writing

Underline each verb. Circle each subject. Make sure that every clause has a subject and a verb.

Check that every verb has the correct tense.

Check that all direct quotations are inside quotation marks.

Run the spell checker on your computer. If you are still not sure of the correct spelling of a word, use a dictionary.

Check that you have punctuated sentences correctly.

Review your editing card to be sure that you have not repeated errors from your previous paragraphs. Remember, your peer reader and your instructor should not be grammar editors; you should be your own grammar editor.

EXERCISE 11 Doing a peer response

Exchange your paragraph with another student. Using Peer Response Form 3-1 (p. 202), review the new paragraph. Remember, the most important reason to do a peer review is not for someone else to review your paragraph but for you to learn how to edit writing.

Are there sentences in your classmate's paragraph that confuse you? Perhaps that is because there is a grammar problem. Can you suggest a correction? Even if you cannot decide how to improve your classmate's errors, you will be helping yourself (and your classmate) by recognizing and noting confusing sentences.

Don't just look for problems! See what you find interesting in the paragraph. Notice vocabulary words that you would like to use in your own writing. If you like something, make a note of it for yourself and be sure to tell your classmate.

EXERCISE 12   **Revising your paragraph**

Reread the assignment. Then reread the draft of your paragraph. Does your paragraph fulfill the assignment?

Consider the comments your peer reviewer made. Also, think of what you observed when you reviewed your partner's paragraph. (Remember, the most important part of the peer response activity is what <u>you</u> learn about editing.) What did you like about that paragraph? What confused you? What changes can you make to improve your paragraph?

> ► Do you want to add more specific details? Be sure that any new details are placed with the correct major point.
> ► Do you want to change the order of the sentences?
> ► Do you want to combine some sentences?
> ► Have you used appropriate transition words?

Rewrite your paragraph if necessary.

Submit your paragraph to your instructor. Be sure to attach Peer Response Form 3-1 and your editing card to your paragraph.

EXERCISE 13   **Updating your editing card**

When your instructor returns your paragraph, note any new errors on your editing card. If an old error is listed that you did not make in this chapter, cross out that error on the card. (Do not forget about this type of error, but because you now have control over it, you should not be making it again.)

EXERCISE 14   **Rewriting your paragraph**

If necessary, rewrite your paragraph. Place your revised paragraph in your folder.

Writing Assignment 2

Write a paragraph explaining how an occupation fits or does not fit a specific person's personality. To complete this assignment, you will interview a person and then report the information that you learn. Follow the steps of Gathering Information; Focusing and Organizing; and Writing, Editing, and Revising.

▷ Gathering Information

U.S. Department of Labor
Bureau of Labor Statistics
Occupational Outlook Handbook

Food and Beverage Serving and Related Workers

Nature of the Work | Working Conditions | Employment | Training, Other Qualifications, and Advancement | Job Outlook | Earnings | Related Occupations | Sources of Additional Information

SIGNIFICANT POINTS

Hosts and hostesses try to create a good impression of a restaurant by warmly welcoming guests. Because hosts and hostesses are a restaurant's personal representatives, they try to ensure that service is prompt and courteous and that the meal meets expectations. They may courteously direct patrons to where coats and other personal items may be left and indicate where patrons can wait until their table is ready. Hosts and hostesses assign guests to tables suitable for the size of their group, escort patrons to their seats, and provide menus. They also schedule dining reservations, arrange parties, and organize any special services that are required. In some restaurants, they also act as cashiers.

(Source: From http://www.bls.gov/oco/ocos162.htm)

EXERCISE 15 Using your judgment

Read the job description of food and beverage servers, and check all the personality factors that would best match this job.

_____ Likes to interact with people   _____ Manages time well

_____ Annoyed by interruptions   _____ Notices little details

_____ Enjoys surprises   _____ Prefers to work alone

_____ Easily distracted   _____ Avoids responsibility

_____ Always tactful   _____ Dislikes indoor work

WEB POWER

Visit the website for this text at
http://esl.college.hmco.com/students for a listing of links
that offer information about personality styles. In small
groups, discuss the most interesting information that you
find. Do you and the members of your group agree with
the website information? Why or why not?

EXERCISE 16 Freewriting

Freewrite for five minutes about how your own personality traits would relate to different work situations. For example, do you like to work with people, or alone? Do you find a fast-paced schedule stimulating, or exhausting? Do you work well or poorly under time pressure? Write as much as you can without stopping. Do not worry about making mistakes. Instead, put all your ideas on paper.

EXERCISE 17 Discussing with your classmates

On the basis of what you know about personality styles, list on the board at least five enjoyable and five disagreeable parts of three of the following occupations: restaurant hostess, pilot, salesperson, firefighter, teacher, dentist. Do all the students agree? Why or why not?

EXERCISE 18 **Setting up the interview**

Choose someone who has an occupation that interests you to interview.
You could interview a family member or a friend, a coworker or your boss.
You could find a company in a field that interests you and ask to interview
someone in the company.

Make an appointment. While an in-person meeting is best (remember
the eye contact and body language used during the oral presentations),
a telephone interview or an e-mail exchange can also work.

Tell the person that you would like to meet for only fifteen to twenty
minutes.

EXERCISE 19 **Preparing for the interview**

First, decide whom you will interview. Look up the person's occupation in
the Occupational Outlook Handbook *(located on the Web or perhaps in*
your college counseling center), and read the information. Take notes on
some of the information that interests or confuses you. This will help you
prepare for your interview.

EXERCISE 20 **Reviewing the interview outline**

With a partner, review the interview outline on page 105.

Add or change questions on the outline, depending on your interviewee's
occupation. Remember: use the notes you took from the Occupational
Outlook Handbook *to guide your modification of the interview outline.*
The goal is to see how well the person's personality fits her or his chosen
occupation.

Practice the interview by role-playing: one student pretends to be the
interviewee while her or his partner asks the questions and takes notes on
the responses.

Switch roles.

Keep your notes clear! In your report, you will present the information and ideas of the person you interviewed. If you intend to quote the person's words exactly as the person said them, you must be sure to write exactly those words in your notes. Enclose the speaker's exact words in quotation marks ("…") so that when you are writing the report, you will remember when you are using another person's words.

Interview Questions

Person's Name: _____   Occupation: _____

Employer: _____   Job Title: _____

1. Please describe what you usually do during a workday.

(If the person you are interviewing does not provide many details, ask some follow-up questions. Refer to the freewriting you did and ask some questions from that information, or try some of these: *What was the first thing you did when you got to work this morning? Do you spend most of your workday working alone or with other people? What types of deadlines do you have in your job? Do you have a lot of paperwork in your job? Do you do a lot of hands-on work in your job? What type of guidance or directions do you receive?*)

2. What do you like best about your job? Why?

3. What would you like to see changed in your job? Why?

4. If you could make your career choice all over again, would you choose the same occupation? _____ Why or why not?

5. When did you first think of following this career path?

6. Do you think your occupation fits your personality? Why or why not?

EXERCISE 21   Having the interview

Arrive on time. Be prepared with your questions. Know the correct pronunciation and spelling of the person's name!

Have a pencil and paper ready. It can be very difficult to write down all the words that a person is saying. If you are not able to write down the exact words, you can still report on the information and ideas in your own words as long as you give credit to the person for the information. (You could ask if the person would be willing to let you audiotape the interview, but some people find taping uncomfortable.)

EXERCISE 22   Sending a thank-you note

After the interview, send a short thank-you note in which you thank the person for meeting with you, and mention something you particularly appreciated learning.

POWER GRAMMAR

Direct Quotations/Reported Speech

A direct quotation contains the exact words said by a person. Reported speech contains the exact information but not the exact words said by a person.

In a direct quotation, the speaker's words are inside quotation marks (" ... ").
Notice the comma **after** the verb *said* and the period **inside** the quotation marks.

Mr. Nguyen said, "Each day I find my work very tough and interesting."

If you want to report the same information in your own words, you need to change the words and the punctuation. You must still give credit (cite) the person who gave the information.

Mr. Nguyen said that he thought his job was demanding but fascinating every day. There are no quotation marks. There is no comma after the words *Mr. Nguyen said.*

If you want to quote only a part of a sentence, be sure that the words the person actually spoke are inside quotation marks.

Mr. Nguyen said that he found his job "very tough and interesting" every day.

EXERCISE 23 Transitioning from quoted speech

Read the middle example in the Power Grammar box on page 106, and fill in the blanks below:

▶ There is no comma after the verb *said*. The word *that* shows you are reporting what Mr. Nguyen said but (are, are not)

_____ using his exact words.

▶ The pronoun changed from *I* to *he*. Why?

_____

▶ The verb tense changed from present (*find*) to past (*found*). Why?

_____

▶ There are no quotation marks. Why?

_____

EXERCISE 24 Working in pairs

Review your answers to Exercise 23 with a partner.

EXERCISE 25 Changing from quoted to reported speech

With a partner, change the sentences below to reported speech. Use a dictionary or thesaurus to find synonyms for some of the words in the quotations.

1. Ms. Sada said, "I enjoy constructing window displays."

   Ms. Sada said that _____

   _____

2. Prof. O'Neill stated, "Being a teacher is essential work. However, it

   can be difficult." _____

   _____

3. Mr. Rylanz answered, "The thing I like least about my job is that I have to get up so early every morning. I really don't like that."

   _____

   _____

   _____

▽ Focusing and Organizing

EXERCISE 26 Reviewing a chart

Review the following chart, and circle the personality trait that does not match the job description.

A personality and a job		
Alexandra ("Alex") Garcia-Hilar	Matches = Doesn't match ≠	*Restaurant hostess*
Likes working with people *"I have to be fun-loving because of the environment I am in; it's like being at a party."* A hostess must be "outgoing, spontaneous, fun-loving, interactive, positive, and polite."	=	**Direct contact with people** The hostess greets every person who comes to the restaurant. Seats them, gives menus, answers questions, and answers phone.
Is positive She likes "to talk to other employees and guests. I also need to be able to handle many tasks and people at once, with a positive attitude, and I think I do."	=	**Must always make people feel good** The owners want people to come back again. The resaurant has to feel upbeat.
Is polite "The customer is always right! And if I can make them think they are right, I can get larger tips."	=	**Must be courteous** The hostess is the restaurant's representative and her job is to make sure the diners always feel welcome.
Is spontaneous Likes having things different all the time. Would hate to work "in a boring office."	=	**Has to handle all sorts of things** She has to respond to a lot of unplanned things. People have lost car keys, babies cry and spoil dinner for people, a waiter once dropped a big tray of food and drinks all over the floor, someone once left without paying …
Does not like the preopening work *For an hour before the place opens, she has to do a bunch of chores by herself. It's not a big part of her job though.*	≠	**Has to set up the restaurant every night** Check reservations, set up tables, type up menus …

EXERCISE 27 Reading a student sample

Read Student Sample 2, and notice the organization of the information.

Topic Sentence
with Controlling Idea

First Major Point

Supporting Details

Second Major Point

Supporting Details

Third Major Point

Supporting Details

Contrasting
Information

Transition Back to
Positive

Concluding
Sentence

Student Sample 2

Alexandra Garcia-Hilar, the hostess at the Cottage House Restaurant, loves her job because she loves to work with people, which is what a hostess does. When guests arrive, she seats them, gives them menus, and answers any questions they might have. She also answers the phone during the evening and handles any problems that arise. She has helped people find their car keys, quieted crying babies, and cleaned up after a waiter dropped an entire tray of food. Alex thinks a hostess must be "outgoing, spontaneous, fun-loving, interactive, positive, and polite." When describing her outgoing and spontaneous side, she said that she liked "to talk to other employees and guests. I also need to be able to handle many tasks and people at once, with a positive attitude, and I think I do." She then went on to say, "My job is fun because it's like being at a party every night." She would not want to sit behind a desk all day. Alex's love of people and her positive attitude fit her job because she has to talk to many different people and create an environment where people want to come back to eat again. The most important trait is to be polite, and she always is. When Alex was talking about politeness, she exclaimed, "The customer is always right! And if I can make them think they are right, I can get larger tips." The only part of Alex's job that she does not like is the hour before the restaurant opens when she has to check reservations, help set tables, and type up menu changes. However, overall, Alex's job seems to fit her personality like a glove.

EXERCISE 28 Comparing a chart to a final paragraph

Review the chart on page 108 and Student Sample 2. Read the paragraph's first point and its supporting details, and underline this information in the chart. Repeat this process for the second and third points and for the contrasting information.

EXERCISE 29 Completing your chart

Using the information in your interview notes, complete the following chart.

A Personality and a Job		
	Matches =	
	Doesn't match ≠	

EXERCISE ▪ 30 ▪ **Choosing major points and specific details**

Decide what major points and specific details you will include in your paragraph.

Review the information in your chart (p. 110) and decide whether, in your opinion, the personality of your interviewee and her or his occupation are a good match.

Identify two to four major points *that will support this opinion.*

Enter these major points in the chart below. Put the most important point first if one point is more important than the others.

Add specific details to each major point. Use examples or quotations from the person you interviewed.

Major Point #1   Specific Details
Major Point #2   Specific Details
Major Point #3   Specific Details
Major Point #4   Specific Details

POWER GRAMMAR

Identifying Nouns

When you use a person's words or ideas in an academic report, you must identify (cite) the person the first time you mention her or him. In this report, you need to identify the person's name and job.

To give additional information about a noun (or a noun phrase), place a comma after the original noun and add the identifying information. Follow the information with another comma.	Julia Hilar, a travel agent with Flights of Fancy Travel Service, said that because the most important quality of a good travel agent is …
Notice that, in these examples, the identifying information is not a clause; it is a phrase: a group of words without a verb.	Mr. Santee Gala, the personnel manager of Bloomington Manufacturing, has always loved working with people, so …

Dr. Sasha Greelin, a local pediatrician, expressed the opinion that the training for … |
| If, in a different report, you want to emphasize the occupation rather than the person, you could switch the phrases. | The chief real estate broker at Homes United Realty, Ms. Estella Jareau, warned that the job outlook …

The real estate attorney at Homes United Realty, Ms. Camila Palais, however, continues to feel … |
| An adjective clause is also grammatically correct. | Julia Hilar, <u>who is a travel agent with Flights of Fancy Travel Service</u>, said that because the most … |

EXERCISE 31 Identifying people

Finish the sentences by filling in the names and identifying information from the business cards.

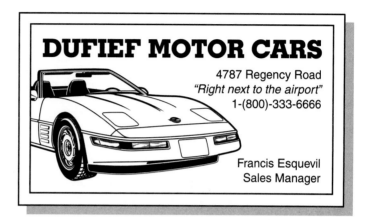

DUFIEF MOTOR CARS

4787 Regency Road
"Right next to the airport"
1-(800)-333-6666

Francis Esquevil
Sales Manager

1. _____

_____

has been working in sales for more than twenty-five years.

Networking News

www.networkingnews.com

Need a job? We can help!

Shirlee Pylor
Website Manager
spylor@getajob.com

2. _____

_____

used to work in a downtown office but now works from home.

EXERCISE 32 **Identifying your interviewee**

Write two sentences about the person you interviewed:

1. In this sentence, use an identifying phrase after the name of the interviewee.

   _____

   _____

2. In this sentence, use the person's name after her or his occupation.

   _____

   _____

POWER GRAMMAR

Present Perfect Tense

Academic writers frequently link past information to a current situation.

This writer started his paragraph by connecting past events to present events. This sentence structure can be used by other writers—like you!

Since the very first members of Mr. Piazza's family <u>arrived</u> in the United States from Italy, they <u>have been</u> businesspeople.

Past tense is used when an action or situation is in the past. Past tense does not make a connection to present time. The writer used past tense to tell about things that happened in the past.

His great grandfather <u>was</u> a farmer, and he <u>used to sell</u> his products in the public market. After him, his grandfather, his father, and all his uncles <u>worked</u> in some kind of business.

The **present perfect tense** identifies a period of time that began in the past but that has not yet ended.

Beginning time in the past: the very first members of his family <u>arrived</u> in the United States from Italy.
Verb to make connection to present time: they <u>have been</u> businesspeople.

EXERCISE 33 Identifying verb tenses

Circle the past tense verbs. Underline the present perfect tense verbs. The first one has been done for you.

1. *Because her family never doubted her dream of becoming a teacher, Ms. Pacaleft has never doubted her decision to quit her clerical job and return to school.*
2. *The photographer has not yet begun to process the film that he shot yesterday.*
3. *Ever since I was a child, I have always loved music.*
4. *Since my brother became a geriatric nurse, he has become much more understanding of people's fears and concerns.*
5. *The radio announcers have attended additional training sessions since they began working here a month ago.*

EXERCISE 34 Answering a question

With a partner, review the sentences in Exercise 33. Answer this question: How is present perfect tense constructed?**

_____

_____

_____

_____

W E B   P O W E R

Visit the website for this text at
http://esl.college.hmco.com/students for a listing of
irregular past participles and a list of links that offer
present perfect tense practice activities.

**Answer: To construct present perfect tense, use the present tense of the verb *to have* and the past participle (which is usually the -*ed* form) of the main verb.

EXERCISE 35 **Constructing the present perfect tense**

Fill in the blanks with the present perfect tense of one of the following verbs:
debug, learn, offer, study, upload, write, research, interview.

Select a verb that makes sense in each sentence. The list contains an extra
verb, so read the sentences carefully to get the correct meaning.

1. Dr. Biangi, a professor at the community college, _____

   several textbooks. He uses information from his students to make his

   books more useful.

2. Since the beginning of the school year, the librarians _____

   several new tutorials onto the website. Last year, they provided ten

   tutorials on English grammar and punctuation.

3. The career counselors _____ weekly workshops for students

   for the past two months. These workshops help students find

   information about careers.

4. My friend started classes in information systems last month. Since

   then, she _____ a lot about databases and the Internet.

5. The computer science students _____ several computer

   languages since the beginning of the semester.

6. The personnel manager at Current Traders _____

   14 applicants so far this week.

7. Do not make a final decision about your career until you

   _____ the training requirements and the job outlook.

SPOTLIGHT ON WRITING SKILLS

Written Speech Is Different from Oral Speech

Oral Form	Written Form	Important Points
Ayn: ***Haven't*** seen you in a while. *How you been?*	***I have not*** seen you in a while. ***How have*** you been?	Many people pronounce *been* and *being* alike, so writers must carefully edit their work to be sure they have written the correct word.
Anton: ***Doing*** OK. ***Been*** really busy with school and work. My ***father's being*** really strict about my grades, too.	***I have been doing*** OK. ***I have been*** really busy with school and work. My ***father is being*** really strict about my grades, too.	In conversational speech, it is appropriate to leave out words that must be included in writing.
He***'s working*** as a pilot for a new airline.	He **is working** as a pilot for a new airline.	Because *has* and *is* are pronounced exactly alike when they are contracted in conversational speech, the verb tense is sometimes not obvious to the listener.
She***'s flown*** jet planes since she joined the air force.	She **has flown** jet planes since she joined the air force.	

Tip: When you are confused about how to write what you have heard, remember—*have* is followed by a past participle, not the *-ing* form of the verb.

     have installed is correct   ~~*have installing*~~ is incorrect

EXERCISE 36   Hearing "Whaddya Say?"

What we hear is not always what we write!

Write the sentences you hear. Write complete verbs.

1. _____

2. _____

3. _____

4. _____

5. _____

✓ Writing, Editing, and Revising

EXERCISE 37   Writing your first draft

Reread Writing Assignment 2 (p. 102). Then use the information you have gathered, focused, and organized to write a first rough draft of your paragraph. Use the checklist to indicate what steps you have completed.

_____ Indent and leave margins on both sides of the page.

_____ Write your topic sentence. Think about the personality of the person you interviewed. How well does the person's personality suit her or his occupation? Write a topic sentence evaluating the "fit" between the personality of the person you interviewed and the occupation. Be sure to include the general reason(s) why you reached this conclusion.

_____ Identify the person by giving her or his complete name and a job description or title.

_____ Develop your supporting ideas in complete sentences.

_____ Review Student Sample 2 (p. 109) and the Power Grammar (p. 106). Be sure to include at least two direct quotations.

_____ Write a concluding sentence for your paragraph. You can restate your topic sentence or perhaps state your feelings about the best personality types for the occupation.

EXERCISE 38 **Rereading your draft**

Follow these steps when rereading your draft:

1. Underline every verb. Circle every subject. Make sure every clause has a subject and a verb.
2. Draw a box around every present perfect tense verb, and be sure you constructed it correctly. Can you explain why you chose to use present perfect tense?
3. Check that you identified the person completely and accurately.
4. If you have used any quotes, check your notes to make sure you have quoted the person accurately.
5. Run spell checker on your computer. If you are still not sure of the correct spelling of a word, use a dictionary.
6. Check your editing card to make sure you are not making the same errors you made in previous paragraphs.

EXERCISE 39 **Doing a peer response**

Exchange your paragraph with a partner. Using Peer Response Form 3-2 (p. 203), review the new paragraph.

EXERCISE 40 **Revising your writing**

Follow these steps as you revise your writing.

1. Reread the assignment (p. 102). Then reread the draft of your paragraph. Have you followed the directions?
2. Consider the comments made by your peer reviewer. Also, think of what you observed when you reviewed your partner's paragraph. What did you like about that paragraph? What confused you? What changes can you make to improve your paragraph?
   ► Does your topic sentence clearly indicate the main idea of your paragraph—how well the occupation fits or does not fit the person's personality?
   ► Do your major points fully support the topic sentence?
   ► Do you have specific details that explain or illustrate the major points?
   ► Is your paragraph interesting?
3. Revise and then rewrite your paragraph.
4. Submit your paragraph to your instructor. Be sure to attach your interview notes, the peer review sheet, and your editing card.

EXERCISE 41 Updating your editing card

When your instructor returns your paragraph, add any new errors you made onto your editing card. If you have gained control over old errors, cross them out on the card. (Good job!)

EXERCISE 42 Rewriting your paragraph

Rewrite your paragraph, if necessary. Place your revised paragraph, all your drafts, and your interview notes in your folder.

▷ Additional Topics for More Practice and Assessment

Additional Writing Assignments

   A. Read a biography of a person who worked in a field that interests you. Write a paragraph explaining the reasons why the person chose to work in the field.
   B. Go to your college's counseling center and find material on a field that interests you. Write a paragraph about what you learned about the field from the materials.
   C. Interview a classmate about her or his career goals. Write a paragraph explaining why the student is interested in the field.

Chapter 3 Self-Assessment

Answer the following questions on a separate sheet of paper and put the sheet into your folder.

   A. Go back to page 89 and check whether you have accomplished the chapter's objectives. List the objectives you think you have accomplished in one column under the heading "Success." List the objectives you still need to practice in another column under the heading "Practice."

   B. Answer these questions:
      1. In your opinion, what are the major differences between oral and written language?
      2. Why is grammatical accuracy important in academic writing?

C. List ten words you have difficulty spelling correctly. Check your spelling in a dictionary.

D. Answer these questions:
   1. What have you learned from doing peer reviews of other students' paragraphs?
   2. What types of errors were the easiest for you to locate in other students' paragraphs? What types of errors were the most difficult for you to locate in other students' paragraphs? Why?
   3. What are the most important things to remember when changing quoted speech to reported speech?
   4. How do you construct present perfect tense?

E. Explain the difference in meaning between these two sentences.
   1. Mr. Bromley was a service manager at a major auto dealership for two years.
   2. Mr. Bromley has been a service manager at a major auto dealership for two years.

F. Write two questions you would like to ask your instructor about the information or the assignments in this chapter.

WEB POWER

You will find additional exercises related to the content in this chapter at http://esl.college.hmco.com/students.

Expressing Opinions

In this chapter, you will move beyond reporting information to expressing and supporting opinions. This support will be based on researched information. The topic in this chapter is smoking, but the skills you will develop can be applied to any topic either in your college classes or in the workplace.

Academic Writing Objectives

In this chapter, you will write at least three paragraphs in which you will express and support your opinion on smoking. While completing these paragraphs, you will:	I have learned this well.	I need to work on this.
Learn how to use multiple citations		
Review facts and statistics and use them to support your opinion		
Use a personal experience to support your opinion		
Complete a case study		
Distinguish between opinion and persuasion		
Write a persuasive paragraph		
Use passive voice correctly		
Distinguish between different word forms		
Use conditional and hypothetical forms		
Participate in a group peer review		

Writing Assignment 1

Write a paragraph expressing and supporting your opinion on cigarette smoking. To complete this assignment, you will review a variety of facts and statistics and choose some to support your opinion.

HERBLOCK'S CARTOON

---from Herblock: A Cartoonist's Life (Times Books, 1998)

Block, H., *The Washington Post*, January 14, 1964.

EXERCISE **1** **Seeing the cartoonist's opinion**

Look at the editorial cartoon above. Tell a partner your answers to these questions:

A. What is the opinion expressed in this editorial cartoon?

B. What details in the cartoon let you know the artist's opinion?

SPOTLIGHT ON WRITING SKILLS

Multiple Citations

Student Sample 1

Topic Sentence with Controlling Idea → Smoking is really harmful to both smokers and to the people around them. Smoking can destroy a smoker's health

First Major Point — since the smoke contains more than 4,000 chemicals.

Supporting Details — (Slothower) Smoking causes many serious diseases, such as lung cancer, emphysema, and heart disease. Since smoking "reduces the effectiveness of the immune system," smokers

Transition to Next Major Point — frequently are ill (Health Edco). In addition to destroying a smoker's health, secondhand smoke can damage other

Second Major Point — people's health, especially children's. One report stated that

Supporting Details — over 15% of children's visits to a doctor and 20% of children's lung infections were caused by secondhand smoke (California EPA). Secondhand smoke can even cause cavities in children since "saliva can counteract the lactic acid, but passive smoking also causes throat inflammation, which leads to mouth breathing, which dries out the mouth" (Kids' Cavities). Smokers

Concluding Sentence — should think of themselves and others and stop smoking now.

References

California EPA. *Final Report: Health Effects of Exposure to Environmental Tobacco Smoke*, September 1997: n. pag.

Health Edco 2000 WRS Group Ltd. *Once You Know the Facts About Smoking*, n. pag.

"Kids' Cavities Linked to Secondhand Smoke." *Washington Post*, March 12, 2003: p. A8.

Slothower, L., "50 Things You Should Know About Tobacco." Santa Cruz, CA: Journeyworks, 1999, Revised 2002: n. pag.

In Chapter 3, you used in-text citations from one source. In this student's paragraph, several sources are cited. For in-text citations, put the initial name from the full citation (and the page number if applicable) inside parentheses after the sentence that contains the source's information. Then list the full citations below the paragraph.

```
WEB POWER
Visit the website for this text at
http://esl.college.hmco.com/students for links that
give information on how to construct citations following
APA and MLA criteria.
```

▷ Gathering Information

EXERCISE 2   Discussing in small groups

In small groups, discuss your opinions on smoking. Do you believe that children should be encouraged not to smoke? Do you think that smoking in public places should be prohibited or restricted? Do you think that smoking is OK?

Write your opinion: _____

_____

_____

_____

Do all the students in your group have the same opinion? If not, write down some of the other students' opinions.

_____

_____

_____

_____

EXERCISE 3   Reviewing facts and statistics

Review the information on the following pages. Does any of this information support your opinion?

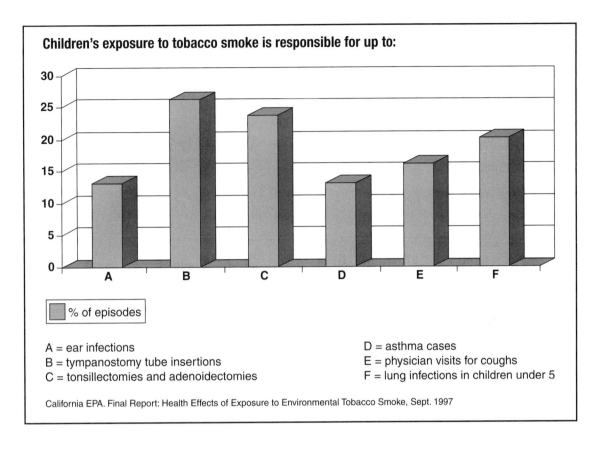

Children's exposure to tobacco smoke is responsible for up to:

% of episodes

A = ear infections
B = tympanostomy tube insertions
C = tonsillectomies and adenoidectomies

D = asthma cases
E = physician visits for coughs
F = lung infections in children under 5

California EPA. Final Report: Health Effects of Exposure to Environmental Tobacco Smoke, Sept. 1997

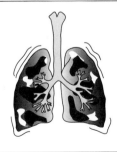

"In addition to cancers, emphysema, and heart disease, smoking causes many other diseases and conditions including strokes, infertility, cavities, bronchitis, and male impotence. Smoking reduces the effectiveness of the immune system, increasing the chance of becoming ill."

Health Edco 2000 WRS Group Ltd., *Once You Know the Facts About Smoking*, n.pag.

Some Statistics:

"Two of the major health effects of cigarette smoking are emphysema and cancer. Emphysema destroys the lung's ability to expand and contract.... [In cancer], damaged cells reproduce rapidly forming clumps of cells called tumors. Tumors steal nutrition and energy from the rest of the body."*

"Overall, nonsmoking wives of husbands who smoke have a 20% increased risk of lung cancer compared with women whose husbands don't smoke."†

"The Environmental Protection Agency estimates that 3,000 nonsmokers die of lung cancer annually—as a result of breathing someone else's cigarette smoke."‡

Forty-nine states and the District of Columbia have some restriction on smoking in public places; Alabama has no state-imposed limits on smoking in public places. These laws range from simple, limited restrictions, such as designated areas in schools, to laws that limit or ban smoking in virtually all public places. Of the states that limit or prohibit smoking in public places, 45 restrict smoking in government workplaces and 24 have extended those limitations to private sector workplaces.∫

"Cigarette smoke has more than 4,000 chemicals in it." (p. 1)

"Cigarette butts are the number one source of pollution on beaches." (p. 3)

"About 70% of people who smoke wish they could quit." (p. 3)

"Eighty percent of smokers started before they were 18 years old." (p. 2)**

"Children who inhale secondhand cigarette smoke have a higher risk of getting cavities in their deciduous, or primary, teeth, researchers said yesterday. ...Tooth decay in children is caused not by sweets, but by a bacterium that produces a lactic acid. Saliva can counteract the lactic acid, but passive smoking also causes throat inflammation, which leads to mouth breathing, which dries out the mouth."††

*American Cancer Society, *The Decision Is Yours*, 1996, n. pag.
†DHHS, 1993, *Smoking and Tobacco Control*, NIH Pub. No. 93-360, Monograph 4. pp. v and vii.
‡American Cancer Society, "The Smoke Around You: The Risks of Involuntary Smoking," 1998. p. 1.
∫ *Here Are Some of the Facts About Smoking*. (2002, June).Retrieved March 17, 2003, from
   http://www.smoke-away.us/facts.htm.
**Slothower, L., "50 Things You Should Know About Tobacco," 1999, Revised 2002. Journeyworks: Santa Cruz,
   CA. n. pag.
†† *Washington Post*, March 12, 2003, p. A8.

Secondhand smoke, or environmental tobacco smoke (ETS),
contains more than forty cancer-causing toxins. ETS has been shown to
harm children's health by causing the problems shown in the figure.

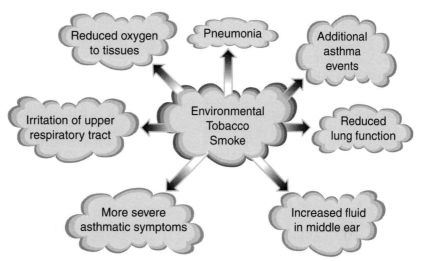

Samet, J. M. (1999, January 7). *Synthesis: The Health Effects of Tobacco Smoke Exposure
on Children.* Retrieved March 20, 2003 from World Health Organization:
http://www5.who.int/tobacco/page.cfm?tld=67

WEB POWER

Visit the website for this text at
http://esl.college.hmco.com/students for links that offer
information on smoking, or use a search engine
(e.g., Google.com, AskJeeves.com) to locate more
information on the issue of smoking.

▽ Focusing and Organizing

EXERCISE 4   Filling in a graphic organizer

*Fill in this graphic organizer. Your opinion on smoking (e.g., smoking in
general, secondhand smoke, smoking and children) is the Main Idea. Your
major points are the general reasons (e.g., Cigarette smoking can harm your
health). The supporting details are the facts or statistics from the preceding
pages or others that you located on your own. Be sure to put complete
citations in the source boxes.*

OPINION _____

General Reason #1

General Reason #2

Supporting Fact/Statistic

Source:

Supporting Fact/Statistic

Source:

Supporting Fact/Statistic

Source:

Supporting Fact/Statistic

Source:

Conclusion _____

POWER GRAMMAR

Figuring Out Passive Sentences

In passive sentences, the subject is the receiver of the action, not the doer.

Most English sentences have three parts: (1) subject, (2) verb, (3) object.

Sentences like these are called "active" sentences.

1   2   3
My uncle smokes cigarettes.

(My uncle does the smoking and the cigarettes receive the action of my uncle.)

In active sentences, the subject is the doer of the action. The object receives the action.

1   2   3
Cigarettes cause health problems.

Sometimes, you want to emphasize the receiver in a sentence, so you move the receiver of the action to the subject position. These sentences are called "passive" sentences.

1   2
Health problems are caused by cigarettes.

(The health problems did not cause themselves.)

In passive sentences, the subject is the receiver of the verb's action, so these sentences have no objects. The doer can be indicated with a "by . . ." phrase.

1   2
Cigarette smoking has been prohibited in restaurants and bars by the town council.

(The smoking did not prohibit itself.)

Passive sentences are used when the receiver of the action is more important than the doer of the action.

1   2
The patient's life was saved by the early diagnosis.

The subject of a sentence is usually the most important item in the sentence, so when the receiver of the action is important, it can become the subject of the verb.

(The patient's life is more important than the diagnosis.)

(Continued)

The topic is the most important thing in a paragraph, so sentences that mention the topic will frequently use the topic as the subject of the sentence. Sometimes that means that a writer will choose passive sentences.

If the paragraph's topic is "secondhand smoke," then that would be the most logical subject for sentences about secondhand smoke.

(Passive)
<u>Secondhand smoke</u> has been found to cause health problems in small children.

Using the topic as the subject of the sentences in a paragraph helps readers understand the focus of the paragraph. Passive sentences are frequently found in scientific writing because the <u>focus</u> of such writing is usually the <u>result</u> of an experiment or research project, not the people who did the work.

If the paragraph's topic is "the National Cancer Institute," then that would be the most logical subject for sentences about the institute.

(Active)
<u>The National Cancer Institute</u> has found that secondhand smoke can cause health problems in small children.

Passive voice is composed of a form of the verb *be* and the past participle of the action verb.

Smoking <u>has been prohibited</u> in schools since 1990.

- ► The verb *be* shows the time and changes tense when the time of the action changes.

Smoking <u>was prohibited</u> in local restaurants last year.

- ► The participle does not change form when the time of the verb changes.

Smoking <u>is prohibited</u> on all airplane flights.

EXERCISE 5 **Locating passive**

Reread Student Sample 1 (p. 125).

Underline the passive verb.

A. Why do you think the writer used a passive verb?

_____

_____

_____

B. Do you think the passive verb is appropriate? Why?

_____

_____

_____

EXERCISE 6 **Recognizing active and passive**

Write Active *or* Passive *after each sentence.*

1. Many American teenagers smoke cigarettes.

_____

2. Cigarette smoking in restaurants should be prohibited.

_____

3. In 2003, millions of cartons of cigarettes were bought in the United States. _____

4. Individuals have a right to smoke if they want to smoke.

_____

5. Cigarette companies spend millions of dollars a year on ads.

_____

6. Every year, millions of dollars are spent on cigarette ads.

_____

EXERCISE **7** **Constructing passive**

Put the verbs in parentheses into passive. Do not change the time of the verbs.

1. People who claim that cigarette smoking <u>made</u> them ill <u>have sued</u> tobacco companies.

    Tobacco companies (sue) _____ by people who

    claim they (make) _____ ill by cigarette smoking.

2. The pediatrician said that the cigarette smoking in the apartment <u>has affected</u> my baby cousin's lungs.

    The pediatrician said that my baby cousin's lungs (affect)

    _____ by the cigarette smoking in the apartment.

3. Many people <u>enjoy</u> cigarette smoking.

    Cigarette smoking (enjoy) _____ by many people.

4. My friend smoked cigarettes to help control her weight.

    Cigarettes (smoke) _____ by my friend to help her

    control her weight.

5. Secondhand smoke aggravates my cousin's asthma.

    My cousin's asthma (aggravate) _____ by

    secondhand smoke.

6. The salesclerks <u>will</u> not <u>sell</u> cigarettes to teenagers in that store.

    In that store, cigarettes (sell, not) _____ to teenagers.

7. Government regulations <u>have restricted</u> the advertising of tobacco products.

    The advertising of tobacco products (restrict) _____

    by government regulations.

▷ Writing, Editing, and Revising

EXERCISE 8 Writing your first draft

Reread Writing Assignment 1 (p. 124). Then use the information in your graphic organizer (p. 130) to write a first, rough draft of your paragraph. Use this checklist to indicate what steps you have completed.

A. _____ Indent the first sentence of the paragraph.

B. _____ Leave margins on both the left and right sides of the page.

C. _____ Write your topic sentence. You may begin your topic sentence with an introductory phrase, such as "In my opinion, . . .," or you may simply state your opinion on smoking.

D. _____ Write sentences that explain the reasons for your opinion (major points).

E. _____ Write sentences that give facts or statistics supporting each reason (specific supporting details).

F. _____ Choose appropriate transition words. Make sure you give your readers signals when you are moving from one major point to the next.
  ▸ Some of the transition words that are appropriate for this type of paragraph are *First, Second, Also, In addition*, and *Additionally*.
  ▸ If one major point is more important than the others, you might use these transition words: *Most important, Next*, and *Also*.

G. _____ Write a concluding sentence for your paragraph that clarifies, summarizes, or restates your opinion.

EXERCISE **9** **Checking your writing**

A. _____ Underline each verb. Circle each subject. Make sure every clause has a subject and a verb.

B. _____ Check every verb to be sure you have the correct tense.

C. _____ Be sure that you have punctuated your sentences correctly.

D. _____ Did you use passive voice? What was your reason for using it?

_____

_____

E. _____ Might passive voice be a better choice in any of the sentences? If so, change the sentence(s) to passive voice.

F. _____ Check that you have put all direct quotations inside quotation marks.

G. _____ Make sure you use signal words that will help your readers understand the logical connection between your ideas.

H. _____ Check that your in-text citations and your references are accurate.

I. _____ Check that any direct quotations are inside quotation marks.

J. _____ Run spell checker on your computer. If you are still not sure of the correct spelling of a word, use a dictionary.

K. _____ Review your editing card to be sure that you have not repeated errors from your previous paragraphs.

EXERCISE **10** **Doing a peer response**

Exchange your paragraph with a partner. Using Peer Response Form 4-1 (p. 204), review the new paragraph.

EXERCISE 11   Revising your paragraph

Reread the assignment (p. 124). Then reread the draft of your paragraph. Does your paragraph fulfill the assignment? Did you express an opinion supported by facts or statistics?

Consider the comments made by your peer reviewer. Also, think of what you observed when you reviewed your partner's paragraph. What did you like about that paragraph? What confused you? What changes can you make to improve your paragraph?

- ► Have you explained the reasons for your opinion clearly?
- ► Do you want to add more specific details, such as facts or statistics? Be sure that any new details are placed with the correct major point.
- ► Did you give citations for all your sources of information?
- ► Have you used appropriate transition words?

Rewrite your paragraph.

Submit your paragraph to your instructor. Be sure to attach the peer response form and your editing card to your paragraph.

EXERCISE 12   Updating your editing card

When your instructor returns your paragraph, note on your editing card any new errors. If you did not make an error that is already listed on your editing card (Good job!), cross off that error.

EXERCISE 13   Rewriting your paragraph

If necessary, rewrite your paragraph. Place your revised paragraph and your drafts in your folder.

Writing Assignment 2

Write a paragraph expressing and supporting your opinion on cigarette smoking in public places, such as restaurants and shopping malls. To complete this assignment, you will write a paragraph expressing your opinion and support your opinion with a personal experience.

▽ Gathering Information

EXERCISE 14 Reading a student sample

Student Sample 2

Topic Sentence with Controlling Idea

Background Information

First Event

Second Event

Third Event

Current Situation

Concluding Sentence

A person who smokes cigarettes or cigars in public places can have dangerous effects on nonsmokers' health. My friend Mai worked in a restaurant where smoking was allowed. Many of the customers smoked, so she had to inhale that smoke all day. One day, while she was working, she suddenly had a breathing problem, and had to be taken to the hospital. The doctor who treated her told her that if she continued working at that place where she had to breathe cigarette smoke, she would have a disease such as lung cancer. The doctor advised her to quit her job, so she left that job and now is working in a library. Her health has improved although she sometimes still has breathing problems. It is a matter of life and breath, so in my opinion, smoking in public places must stop.

EXERCISE 🔢 Labeling a student sample

Student Sample 2 (on page 138) was labeled. Notice how the events are in chronological (time) order. Label Student Sample 3, which is also written in chronological order, by drawing arrows to the correct part of the student's paragraph.

Student Sample 3

Topic Sentence with
Controlling Idea

Background
Information

First Event

Second Event

Third Event

Current Situation

Concluding
Sentence

Smoking in public places can influence others to smoke and affect their lives badly. My brother Roger, who is 21 years of age, has been smoking for the past five years. He was influenced by his friends to smoke, which caused him to skip school and drop out of high school, all because he thought it was cool. My brother told me that he and his friends had seen other kids smoking on school grounds and in the shopping malls, so they wanted to have a taste. Some of Roger's friends stole cigarettes from their parents and took them to school, so they could share them with their friends. Eventually, they got so addicted that they started to skip school to smoke. Nowadays, my brother tells me that he wishes he had gotten help at the right time, so he would not have dropped out of high school and wasted his money on cigarettes because now none of his high school friends are with him. They all went on their own ways. In my opinion, I think we should have a new law saying that people who smoke in public in front of children could be arrested because the children can be influenced to smoke and then ruin their futures.

EXERCISE 16   **Figuring out verbs**

Reread Student Sample 2 (p. 138), and answer the following questions:

1. Locate the sentence "Her health has improved although she
    sometimes still has breathing problems." Why did the writer choose

    to use present perfect tense? _____

    _____

2. Locate one passive verb, and write it on this line: _____

    _____

3. Why do you think the writer chose to use passive? _____

    _____

4. Do you agree with the choice? Why? _____

    _____

EXERCISE 17   **Figuring out verbs**

Reread Student Sample 3 (p. 139), and answer the following questions:

1. Underline the present perfect tense verb at the beginning of the
    paragraph.

2. The present perfect tense is connecting the present time (Roger is now

    21 years old) to what past time? _____

3. Underline the two passive verbs in the paragraph. Why do you think

    the writer chose to use passive? _____

    _____

    _____

4. Do you agree with the choices? Why? _____

    _____

    _____

EXERCISE 18 Freewriting

Spend five minutes writing about your personal experiences with smoking in public places. What events do you remember in your family, in school, at work, or in a shopping mall or restaurant? Write any information that you remember about these incidents. Don't worry about spelling, punctuation, organization, or grammar. Just write and don't stop for five minutes!

▷ Focusing and Organizing

EXERCISE 19 Choosing one experience

Review your freewriting. Choose one incident that you think most strongly influenced your opinion about smoking in public places.

Now focus on that incident. Think of details from that time. Where were you? Who else was there? What was the weather or time of day? Can you remember colors, smells, sounds or conversations? Write down as many details as you can remember.

EXERCISE 20 Completing a graphic organizer

Fill in the graphic organizer on page 142 with information from this incident.

Choose details from Exercise 19 that will help to clearly tell the story. Some of the details from Exercise 19 might not be relevant. Leave them out. Add other details if necessary.

BACKGROUND

Who was present? _____

Where did this occur? _____

When did this occur? _____

What adjectives describe the feelings of people during this event?

Are the verbs in the correct tense? Do all the verbs have subjects?

What happened first?

Then what happened?

Next?

Next?

What was the end of the incident?

How did this incident affect the writer's thinking about smoking?

SPOTLIGHT ON WRITING SKILLS

Distinguish between Two Different Word Forms

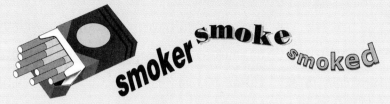

The correct spelling of different forms of a word can be difficult for ear learners of English because it is often difficult to distinguish the slight difference in pronunciation. It is essential, however, to use the correct form in written English.

SMOKER is a noun referring to a person. SMOKED is a verb form. If a writer puts a noun where a verb should be, the sentence will not make sense. Some writers will use dictionaries to check the correct spelling of word forms. This is a good idea, but it can be time-consuming. Writers who become familiar with the word endings for different word forms will have an easier time writing.

As you read, notice word form endings. When you learn new vocabulary, practice the different word forms (noun, verb, adjective, adverb) for each new word. In the next activity, pay attention to the pronunciation of the word forms and their functions in the sentences. Make a note of the different word endings and which word form matches the different word endings.

EXERCISE 21   Hearing "Whaddya Say?"

What we hear is not always what we write!

Write the sentences you hear. Write complete verbs.

1. The restaurant's customers disag_____ with the new city regula_____ on smoking. The disag_____ became so heated that many regu_____ customers went to the City Council meeting and demanded that the Council stop regu_____ smoking. The situation became so disag_____ that the Council stopped the meeting.

2. My cousin's announcement that he was quit_____ smok_____was surpris_____ to me. I was surpris_____ because I had not known that he was a smok_____.

3. Although I consider myself to be a toler_____ person, the situation at my workplace has become intoler_____ for me. My boss will not toler_____ any smoking, even outside the building!

4. Usu_____, there are a lot of students smoking outside the library. However, this morning it was unusu_____ cold, so they would not stand outside in the usua_____ place.

5. Although most instruc_____ are aware of the state legisla_____'s new legisla_____ on smoking in public places, they think that the legisla_____ wording of recent reports is non-instruc_____.

6. Legal exper_____ have advised the campus to expan_____ its smoking areas. There has been a lot of criticism of this exper_____ advice by people who feel the expan_____ will send the wrong message. The legal exper_____ conflicts with the medical advice.

▷ Writing, Editing, and Revising

EXERCISE 22 Writing your first draft

Reread Writing Assignment 2 (p. 138). Then use the information from your graphic organizer (p. 142) to write your paragraph. Use the checklist to indicate what steps you have completed.

A. _____ Remember to indent and to leave margins on both sides of the page.

B. _____ Write your topic sentence, which should express your opinion on smoking in public places.

C. _____ Following the sequence in your graphic organizer, tell about the experience that influenced your opinion.

D. _____ Make sure you give your readers signals when you are moving from one part of the event to the next. Transition words that are appropriate for this type of paragraph include *First, Second, Then, Next, Immediately, Later, Eventually, Finally,* and *At last.*

E. _____ Write a concluding sentence that explains how this event influenced your opinion on smoking in public places.

EXERCISE 23 Rereading your draft

A. _____ Underline every verb. Circle every subject. Make sure that every clause has a subject and a verb.

B. _____ Check every verb to be sure you have the correct tense. Because this is a story, the verbs must tell the sequence of time correctly.

C. _____ If you chose to use passive voice, did you construct it correctly?

D. _____ Make sure you have signal words that will help your readers understand the time sequence in your story.

E. _____ Run spell checker on your computer. If you are still not sure of the correct spelling of a word, use a dictionary.

F. _____ Check your editing card to make sure that you are not making the same errors that you made in previous paragraphs. Write down on your paper, below your paragraph, the types of errors that you particularly looked for while you were editing.

EXERCISE 24 Doing a peer response

Exchange your paragraph with another student. Using Peer Response Form 4-2 (p. 206), review the new paragraph.

EXERCISE 25 Revising your writing

Reread the assignment (p. 138). Then reread the draft of your paragraph. Did you support your opinion on smoking in public places with a personal experience?

Consider the comments made by your peer reviewer. Also, think of what you observed when you reviewed your partner's paragraph. What did you like about that paragraph? What confused you? What changes can you make to improve your paragraph?

- ▶ Have you explained how this incident affected your opinion?
- ▶ Do you want to add more details (e.g., adjectives or adjective clauses) that describe the people or places in the story?
- ▶ Have you used appropriate transitions?
- ▶ Is your story interesting?

Revise and then rewrite your paragraph.

Submit your paragraph to your instructor. Be sure to attach your interview notes, the peer response sheet, and your editing card.

EXERCISE 26 Updating your editing card

When you receive your paragraph back from your instructor, add to your editing card if you made any new types of errors. If you did not make an error that is already listed on your editing card (Good job!), cross off that error. Add your paragraph and your drafts to your folder.

**Master
Student Tip**

Student Sample 4 on the next page was written in response to the case study activity that follows. Because learning in college stresses critical thinking over simple memorization of facts, case studies are used in many disciplines to enable students to work with the content of a course as they will work with the information in their careers.

SPOTLIGHT ON WRITING SKILLS

Opinion and Persuasion

A writer may express an opinion on an issue without promoting any specific action. In other instances, a writer will try to influence readers to change their own opinions on a topic or to take some sort of action related to the topic. Persuasive writing includes your own opinion but goes beyond just expressing it.

Persuasive writing is an important form of writing, not only in school but in all aspects of life. When you are in a career, you will frequently want to influence other people's actions, e.g., convince your supervisor to promote you, persuade a client to hire you, influence your co-workers to participate in a project. Outside of work, you might find yourself trying to convince a legislator to vote for a law or your insurance company to pay an accident claim.

Persuasive writing must be clear and powerful. Your readers will be influenced not by a simple statement of your opinion but by the quality of the support you give for your opinion.

In Chapter 2, you reported other people's opinions on birth order. You did not try to influence your readers to change their own opinion or to act differently towards firstborn children. You simply shared opinions. In Writing Assignment I in this chapter, you expressed your own opinion on the topic of smoking, but you did not attempt to persuade your readers to perform a specific act. In Writing Assignment II, you related a story about an incident that influenced your opinion on smoking in public places, but you did not focus on persuading people to do something specific.

In the next Writing Assignment, you will write a persuasive paragraph in which you will try to influence your readers' attitudes and persuade them to take a specific course of action. Remember, your readers will not be persuaded to do anything if you only state your opinion. You have to convince them by giving clear, well thought-out reasons for them to take action.

EXERCISE 27 Locating opinion and persuasion statements

Read Student Sample 4, and circle two clauses that express the writer's opinion on the topic. Underline the one clause that states the specific action that the writer is encouraging the reader to take.

Student Sample 4

Topic Sentence with
Controlling Idea

"Pro" Statements

Transition to "Con"
Statements

"Con" Statements

Concluding
Sentence

As a resident and voter in the town of Glynwood, I want to spend the $500,000 from the tobacco settlement on the farmers because growing tobacco is the root of all tobacco problems. If the farmers get the money, they will be able change their farming to safe crops, like soybeans and corn. This would be the best way to spend the money because if farmers stopped growing tobacco, cigarette costs would increase and they would be so expensive that many people could not afford them and would have to quit smoking. By the time most farmers stop growing tobacco, there will not be any tobacco products, and if there is not any tobacco, there will not be any tobacco induced diseases, such as lung cancer, heart disease, etc. In contrast, other groups that want the money, such as the hospital and the patients with lung cancer will not eliminate tobacco problems in the future. If we gave them the money, it would only benefit people who already have problems. Even the schools would not be able to eliminate smoking. Growing tobacco is the root cause of the tobacco-induced diseases and if we cut this root, there will be no problems, so vote to spend the money on the farmers.

Why do you think the writer wrote more information in the "Pro" statements than in the "Con" statements?

_____

_____

_____

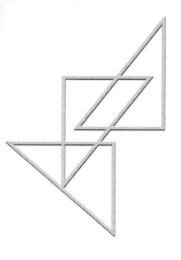

Writing Assignment 3

Write a persuasive paragraph that will convince your readers to give $500,000 to a specific group of people. To complete this assignment, you will participate in a case study activity and write your paragraph in response to this activity.

▷ Gathering Information

EXERCISE 28 Completing a case study

Case Study

Background: In the 1990s, states started suing tobacco companies to recover expenses that resulted from tobacco-caused illnesses. In 1997 and 1998, a nationwide settlement with the tobacco companies was reached. The companies agreed to pay states $246 billion over twenty-five years. States will distribute money to localities for various programs related to smoking.

Activity: You are a resident and voter in the town of Glynwood. Your town has received $500,000 from the settlement, and it is up to the voters to determine how it will be spent.

Complete the case study by following these steps:

A. Read the proposals below and decide how you want to see the money spent.

Hospital: The county hospital is located in Glynwood. It serves more than 6,500 families in the county, including the 3,000 families in the town. The hospital would like to spend the money on specialized equipment to treat emphysema and asthma, both serious medical conditions that have been linked to cigarette smoke. The hospital estimates that this equipment could be used in 275 cases this year. Currently, the nearest hospital with this type of equipment is one hundred miles away. If the hospital had this equipment, it would mean that patients could be treated near their homes, so they and their families would not have to spend the time and money traveling to another county to get treatment.

Patients with Lung Cancer: Fifty families in the town have members with lung cancer, which the families believe was caused in most cases by smoking or exposure to secondhand smoke. These families would like to share the money equally among themselves. They have testified that their medical expenses related to the care of the lung cancer patients are high and that they have suffered financially because the lung cancer patients have not been able to earn a living as they would have if they were not ill.

Schools: The schools would like to develop and implement a comprehensive youth tobacco prevention campaign. Because research shows that most cigarette smokers start smoking before the age of eighteen, the schools feel strongly that the best way to prevent smoking-caused illnesses is to eliminate teenage smoking. They believe that if the program were implemented, future generations would not face the medical problems that the current generations face.

Farmers: Glynwood is located in a farming community. Tobacco is one of the most important crops grown on local farms. Fifteen family farms have depended on tobacco as a major source of income. These families would like to share the money from the settlement to offset the losses they will suffer if they voluntarily change from farming tobacco to farming other crops. They believe that if they continued to produce tobacco, as they are legally allowed to do, they would not suffer any financial loss.

B. Choose who should get the $500,000. (One rule: the money cannot be divided. You must decide on only one recipient.) Indicate your choice by putting a 1 on the line next to your first choice. Also, indicate your second, third, and fourth choices.

Hospital _____   Patients _____   Schools _____   Farmers _____

C. Divide into groups by your choices. All the students who chose the hospital as most deserving of the money should stand in one corner of the room, the students who chose the patients in another corner, and so on.

D. In these groups, you will have five minutes to decide what your best arguments are for making your choice. Why are you right? Why is your choice better than the others? Select one student who will report on your ideas to the entire class. That student should take notes on the ideas expressed in the group.

E. The student from each group will present the arguments for the choice of the group. After each group reports, any student from another group who is persuaded by the arguments can change groups.

▷ Focusing and Organizing

EXERCISE 29 Stating pros and cons

In the charts below, write down the reasons for (pro) your choice and against (con) the other choices.

Pro

Your choice:_____

List all the reasons **for** your choice:

What is/are the most important reason(s) someone should support your choice?

Con

Why is your choice more deserving than the other choices? List reasons **against** these choices compared with your choice.

POWER GRAMMAR

Conditionals or Hypotheticals

In many areas of academic writing, writers need to discuss things that do not yet exist or that did not happen. A scientist might want to propose an experiment. A sociologist might want to discuss possible effects of a program.

When discussing events that have not yet happened but that might happen, you need to use a **conditional form**.	If the hospital gets the money, the doctors will help many patients recover from serious illnesses.
The verb in the *if* clause is in the present tense, and the verb in the result clause is in the future tense.	(The hospital might get the money, but the hospital has not gotten it yet, so the doctors are not yet helping the patients recover.)
When discussing events that usually happen when a particular condition exists, you need to use this conditional form.	If a family member has asthma, he or she gets treatment at the hospital one hundred miles away. (Whenever a person in a family has asthma, he or she goes to the hospital one hundred miles away. If the person does not have asthma, he or she does not go to the hospital one hundred miles away.)
The verbs in both clauses are in the present tense. The first conditional form refers to present or future events that occur or will occur if a condition (*if* clause) occurs.	
When discussing events that are not true at present, you need to use a different form. The condition (*if* clause) is not real. This is sometimes called the second conditional or a **hypothetical form**.	If the tobacco farmers had the money now, they would be able to pay all their bills. (The tobacco farmers do not have the money now, so they are not able to pay all their bills now.)
The verb in the *if* clause is in past tense, and the verb in the result clause is *would* + base form of the verb.	

(Continued)

In the first conditional, the *if* clause is possible and the result clause might actually happen.	→ If the schools get the $100,000, the students next year will receive information on health programs.
In the second conditional, the *if* clause is impossible or unreal. The result clause is imaginary or hypothetical.	→ If the schools had the $100,000 now, there would be antismoking programs for students in all the high schools this semester.

EXERCISE 30 Locating conditionals and hypotheticals

Reread Student Sample 4 (p. 148). Underline two "real" conditionals and two "unreal" conditionals.

EXERCISE 31 Choosing conditionals and hypotheticals

Circle the correct answers to the questions.

1. Which sentence shows that the meeting has not yet taken place:

   a. I was ill, so I could not go to the city council meeting.
   b. If I feel better, I will go to the city council meeting.

2. What does the following sentence mean? "If I smoked cigarettes, I would smoke ones with filters."

   a. Currently, I smoke cigarettes with filters.
   b. Currently, I do not smoke cigarettes.

3. Which person has an older brother who smokes?

   a. Felicia thinks she would not be a smoker if her older brother did not smoke.
   b. Raine would be a smoker if her older brother were a smoker.

4. Which sentence shows that the person lives with a smoker?

   a. If my roommate smoked, I would ask her to smoke outside.
   b. If my roommate smokes, I ask her to smoke outside.

EXERCISE 32   **Writing conditionals and hypotheticals**

Fill in the blanks with the correct forms of the verbs in parentheses ( ).

1. If the citizens (agree) ＿＿＿＿＿＿ with the mayor, they will give the money to the hospital.

2. If the doctors (have) ＿＿＿＿＿＿ the money from the tobacco settlement, they would purchase some new equipment.

3. If the citizens gave the money from the tobacco settlement to the farmers, the farmers (feel) ＿＿＿＿＿＿ very grateful.

4. If the farmers (continue, not) ＿＿＿＿＿＿ to grow tobacco, they would not need the money from the settlement.

5. If the farmers do not grow tobacco, they (grow) ＿＿＿＿＿＿ other crops instead.

▷ Writing, Editing, and Revising

EXERCISE 33   **Writing your first draft**

Reread Writing Assignment 3 (p. 149). Then use the information you have gathered, focused, and organized to write a first, rough draft of your paragraph. Use this checklist to indicate what steps you have completed.

A. ＿＿＿＿＿＿ Remember to indent and to leave margins on both sides of the page.

B. ＿＿＿＿＿＿ Write a topic sentence that clearly states which group you think should receive the $500,000. The topic sentence should also include a statement of the major reason(s) that would persuade a reader to agree with your choice.

C. ＿＿＿＿＿＿ Use information from the Pro/Con charts (p. 151) to write sentences expressing your major reasons and specific details supporting your choice. You could also give a reason against the other choices.

D. ＿＿＿＿＿＿ Review Student Sample 4 on page 148 and the Power Grammar on page 152.

E. _____   Be sure to use conditional/hypothetical statements when necessary.

F. _____   Use transitions to help your reader understand when you are moving from one major point to another. If your paragraph contains reasons for your choice and reasons against the other choices, did you use a transition word to show the change of ideas from pro to con?

G. _____   Write a concluding sentence that encourages your readers to agree with your choice.

EXERCISE 34   Rereading your draft

A. _____   Underline every verb. Circle every subject. Make sure that every clause has a subject and a verb.

B. _____   Check every verb to be sure you have the correct tense.

C. _____   If you have used any conditional tenses, make sure you used the correct verb form. Are your if clauses real or unreal?

D. _____   Make sure you have signal words that will help your readers understand when you are moving from one reason for your choice to another reason or when you are moving from pro statements to con statements.

E. _____   Run spell checker on your computer. If you are still not sure of the correct spelling of a word, use a dictionary.

F. _____   Review your editing card to be sure that you have not repeated errors from your previous paragraphs.

EXERCISE `35`　**Doing a class review**

Submit your paragraph and your textbook to your instructor. Using one paragraph as a model, your instructor will guide the entire class through the Group Peer Review Sheet (p. 157).

EXERCISE `36`　**Doing small-group reviews**

Your instructor will distribute one student's paragraph and textbook to each small group. In your small group, review one paragraph by using the Group Peer Review Sheet (p. 157). Sign your names in the book of the writer of the paragraph. Take turns filling the following roles:

A. One student reads the directions for the first activity on the review form and signs her or his name on the form. The student should sign her or his name in the book of the writer of the paragraph.

B. Another student completes the activity. Write on the paragraph being reviewed.

C. The other students agree or disagree with the answer. Explain reasons for any disagreements.

D. If there is disagreement with the answer, the student who has read the directions for the activity decides on the correct answer.

E. Pass the book and paragraph to the next student. This student should read the directions for activity #2 and sign her or his name on the form in the writer's book.

F. The other students complete the steps as in the first activity.

G. Continue, taking turns.

H. Each small group will review as many paragraphs as they have time to complete.

Group peer review sheet	
Activity	**Name of student in charge of this activity**
1. Locate the topic sentence. Underline the controlling idea.	
2. How many reasons (major points) does the writer give to support the controlling idea? Write the number in the margin of the paragraph.	
3. Locate the transition words between the major points. Circle them.	
4. Is the paragraph persuasive? Why? Write your answers below the paragraph.	
5. Locate any passive voice verbs. Underline them. Write in the margin any problems with these verbs.	
6. Locate any conditional clauses. Underline them. Write in the margin any problems with these clauses.	
7. Locate the most interesting sentence. Circle it.	
8. If any sentences are confusing or incorrect, place brackets [ ] around them.	

EXERCISE 37 Responding to feedback

When you receive your paragraph and textbook back, review the comments and notations of your reviewers. If you have any questions about an activity, talk with the student who was in charge of the activity.

EXERCISE 38 Revising your writing

Reread the assignment (p. 149). Then reread the draft of your paragraph. Does your paragraph fulfill the assignment? Did you write a persuasive paragraph that will convince readers to support your opinion?

Consider the comments made by your peer reviewer. Also, think of what you observed when you reviewed your partner's paragraph. What did you like about that paragraph? What confused you? What changes can you make to improve your paragraph?

> ► Have you made both pro and con statements?
> ► Have you used appropriate transition words?
> ► Did you include specific details that support your reasons?

Revise and then rewrite your paragraph. Be sure to correct any grammar or spelling errors that you may have made in the draft.

Submit your paragraph and editing card to your instructor.

EXERCISE 39 Updating your editing card

When your instructor returns your paragraph, add any new errors that you made onto your editing card. If you have gained control over old errors, cross them out on the card.

EXERCISE 40 Rewriting your paragraph

Rewrite your paragraph, if necessary. Place your revised paragraph and all your drafts in your folder.

▷ Additional Topics for More Practice and Assessment

Additional Writing Assignments

1. Choose a social issue that concerns you, and write a paragraph expressing your opinion and supporting that opinion with facts or statistics.
2. Choose a social issue that concerns you, and write a paragraph expressing your opinion. Explain what in your own life has influenced your opinion.
3. Choose a social issue, and then locate the website of an organization that has a position on the issue. Write a paragraph explaining the basis of the organization's position.
4. Read a newspaper or magazine story on a social issue, and then write a paragraph that explains the different opinions on the issue.

Chapter 4 Self-Assessment

Answer the following questions on a separate sheet of paper and put the sheet into your folder.

A. Go back to page 123, and check whether you have accomplished the chapter's objectives. List the objectives you believe you have accomplished in one column under the heading "Success." List the objectives you still need to practice in another column under the heading "Practice."

B. Answer these questions:
1. What are some transition (signal) words that writers use to show that the major points in a paragraph are in time order?
2. What are some transition (signal) words that writers use to show that a paragraph contains several major points?
3. What are some transition (signal) words that writers use to show that they are moving from positive reasons to negative reasons for an opinion?
4. If you found another student's writing persuasive, what do you think made it persuasive?
5. If you did not find any other student's writing persuasive, what do you think would have made the writing persuasive?

C. Write the sentences with the correct form of the word *smoke* in the blanks:

> *smoke*   *smoker*   *smoked*   *smoking*

The _____ loved the smell of the_____.

It is frequently difficult to quit _____.

D. What is the difference in meaning between the following sentences?
If I had a pack of cigarettes, I would give a cigarette to you.
If I have a pack of cigarettes, I will give a cigarette to you.

E. Answer these questions:
   1. In what college disciplines would you expect to use a lot of conditional/hypothetical forms? Why?
   2. In your opinion, what are the most important things to remember when writing a conditional/hypothetical sentence?
   3. Which sentence sounds better to you? Why?
      a. Even after the Surgeon General's warning, people purchase thousands of packs of cigarettes in the United States every year.
      b. Even after the Surgeon General's warning, thousands of packs of cigarettes are purchased in the United States every year.
   4. If you were a writing tutor, what would you tell students were the most important things to remember about passive voice?
F. Write two questions that you would like to ask your instructor about the information or the assignments in this chapter.

WEB POWER

You will find additional exercises related to the content in this chapter at http://esl.college.hmco.com/students.

Applying Your Writing Skills

This is the final chapter of this book. In the first chapter, this textbook provided a lot of guidance for your writing activities. As the semester progressed, the explicit guidance decreased as you developed the skills necessary for academic writing. Now, for this last chapter, there will be only a minimal amount of direct guidance. By the end of this chapter, you should feel confident that you can, on your own, write clear, informative, and interesting academic paragraphs.

Chapter Objectives

In this chapter, you will write three paragraphs about an issue at your college that you would like to see improved. While completing these paragraphs, you will:	I have learned this well.	I need to work on this.
Develop and implement an action plan		
Use a variety of types of adjectives		
Use adverbs to make your verbs more interesting and specific		
Use a variety of sentence types		
Recognize different levels of formality in writing		
Write academic paragraphs independently		
Adjust your writing to fit your audience		
Edit your writing independently and effectively		

Writing Assignments 1, 2, 3

In this chapter, you will write three paragraphs about a problem at your college that you wish to solve. Because all the paragraphs are on the same topic, you will gather information for all of them at the same time. Each writing assignment will be explained in detail later in the chapter.

For these assignments, you will choose your own topic to write about and follow the three-step writing process (Gathering Information; Focusing and Organizing; and Writing, Editing, and Revising) with only a limited amount of guidance. If you use what you have learned in the previous chapters, by the end of this chapter you will be writing academic paragraphs independently.

▷ Gathering Information

EXERCISE 1 Answering questions about your college

With a partner, see how many of these questions you can answer:

1. What is the college's website address?
2. Does your college have a student newspaper?
   ▶ What is its name?
   ▶ Where is its office?
3. Who is the chief administrator of your college?
4. Does your college have a Board of Trustees or Board of Governors?
5. Who sets the tuition rate?
6. What hours is the library open?
7. How many parking spaces are available for students on your campus?
8. Where is the bookstore?
9. Are faculty required to hold office hours?
10. Where could you find the answers to any questions that you cannot answer?

EXERCISE 2 Choosing your topic

On the board, list problems at your college that students would like to see solved. For example, perhaps the library is not open on weekends, or the cafeteria does not offer vegetarian selections, or not enough sections of required classes are offered in the evenings, or loud conversations among students in hallways disturb classes.

   A. *In small groups, discuss each item from the following perspectives:*

- ► How many people are affected?
- ► How harmful is the issue to students' academics?
- ► How annoying is it?
- ► How difficult would it be to improve the situation?
- ► Would most students want to see the situation changed?
- ► How important is this issue to the students in this class?

   B. *Choose a problem that you are personally interested in seeing solved. Because this issue will be the basis for all the writing that you will do in this chapter, be sure you really are interested in it. You will enjoy the chapter far more if you are truly interested in the topic you are writing about.*

     Issue I have chosen: _____

   C. *If other students in the class wish to write on the same topic, you could form workgroups to help gather and organize information. However, each student must write her or his paragraphs independently.*

EXERCISE 3 Freewriting

Spend five minutes writing about your issue. Write any ideas that come to you about the topic. Why does this issue bother you? Do you have any ideas for a solution? Maybe you want to list questions that you need to answer. Don't worry about spelling, punctuation, organization, or grammar; you will be the only reader. Just write and don't stop for five minutes!

EXERCISE 4 Developing ideas

Review your freewriting to see what information you want to gather in order to write an academic paragraph describing the problem. Also, review your freewriting to see what possible solutions you have already thought of.

EXERCISE 5 **Reviewing an action plan**

Santo, a student at River Community College, developed this plan. With a partner, review Santo's plan and circle the parts of his plan that you might want to include in your own plan.

I will complete several steps in order to improve the parking situation at this college:

1. Gather information about parking situation:
   a. College website—find out how many students attend here
   b. Student newspaper—look at back issues, see if they have written on the problem
   c. Survey students who drive
      ▸ How serious do they think the parking problem is on a scale of 1 to 10?
      ▸ Have they ever been late to class because of parking?
      ▸ Did the lateness affect their grades? How?
      ▸ Have they ever seen a dangerous situation due to parking problem? What?
   d. Staff in Security (Parking Enforcement)—find out how many parking places, ask about problems, how many reserved spots???

2. Brainstorm solutions
   a. Interview—ask for ideas for solutions
      ▸ 10 Students
      ▸ 3 Staff/Faculty
   b. In class discussions—see what others have found out
   c. Talk to students at other colleges—maybe they have solutions

3. Involve other students
   a. Find out how to submit a paragraph to the student newspaper
   b. Get students to e-mail administration
   c. Petition??? Maybe post in cafeteria???
   d. Rally/Event—Maybe have Student Senate sponsor it???? Need to find out names of officers—student newspaper cover it???

4. Communicate with administration
   a. Find out names, titles, job descriptions
   b. Write a letter

EXERCISE 6 Developing an action plan

Develop an action plan that will enable you to both fulfill the writing assignment for this class and perhaps improve the situation that troubles you. Include the parts of Santo's plan that you liked, but also add ideas that you think would be appropriate at your college.

I will complete several steps in order to _____

_____

_____

1. Gather information:
   a.

   b.

   c.

2. Brainstorm solutions
   a.

   b. In class discussions

   c.

3. Involve other students
   a. Find out how to submit a paragraph to the student newspaper

   b.

   c.

4. Communicate with administration
   a. Find out names, titles, job descriptions
   b. Write a letter
   c.

5. Other activities

EXERCISE **7** **Implementing your plan**

Gather information. If you are working with other students, you could divide up the research work. Some students could gather information on the issue while others gather information on possible solutions. Some students could do a survey while others do interviews. Alternatively, you could all work together to devise interview or survey questions.

▶ If you are getting facts off a website or from a newspaper, be sure to make a note of where you got the information from. (Review p. 93 for citation guidelines.)

▶ If you are interviewing people, prepare your questions before you talk with anyone. (Review p. 104 for interview ideas.)

▶ If you are surveying people, prepare your survey questions and response sheets before you begin. (Review pp. 61–65 for survey techniques.)

SPOTLIGHT ON WRITING SKILLS

College Resources

As a college student, you will need to study and write independently, but that does not mean without support. Your college probably has several resources to support students' writing, whether in English or science or business classes. Frequently these writing resources are located in the library or in a writing center.

Examples of useful resources include:

▶ handbooks for writers, which include charts on how to do citations and checklists on common grammar problems

▶ tutorials on plagiarism and how to avoid it

▶ handouts on punctuation and spelling

▶ study materials for grammar and writing

Colleges often offer tutoring for students. Sometimes this is done in the writing center; other times it could be offered in the counseling center. If your college offers tutoring, take advantage of it.

Some colleges also offer workshops for students on writing and research skills. These workshops might not offer credit, but they can give you some real help in improving your writing and research skills. Some colleges have grammar hotlines and e-mail writing support. Find out about your college.

Writing Assignment 1

Write one paragraph of about 125 words that describes a problem at your college and that explains why you think the problem is important. The audience for this paragraph is your instructor and your classmates. Your paragraph will let your audience understand exactly what the problem is and how serious it is.

▷ Gathering Information

You have already gathered information for this paragraph and the other paragraphs in this chapter by implementing your action plan.

▷ Focusing and Organizing

EXERCISE 8 Developing a graphic organizer

What type of graphic organizer would be appropriate for your paragraph? Remember that the type of organizer you use depends on the information you are presenting, as well as on the type of visual organization you prefer.

▶ If you are presenting information that compares your college with another college, you might want to use a Venn diagram (p. 66).
▶ If you are relating an event, you might want to use a time sequence chart (p. 142).
▶ If you have information that falls into different categories, you might want to use a chart (p. 110).
▶ Some students like outlines (p. 25), while others prefer concept maps (pp. 50–53).

No matter which type of visual organizer you choose, you must begin with your overall idea about the topic. Then make sure that all the information relates directly to that overall idea. Eliminate points that do not help support or clarify your main idea. Add supporting details to explain your major points.

SPOTLIGHT ON WRITING SKILLS

Making Nouns More Interesting

Which is more interesting: *students* or *tuition-paying students?* By itself, the noun *students* is very vague, very general. Adding the description *tuition-paying* adds information and makes the noun more specific. Adding adjectives to nouns makes your writing more powerful and more interesting.

EXERCISE 9 Using adjective form

One feature of written language that ear learners frequently have trouble controlling is the correct ending of a word. An ear learner who has heard a word might be unsure of the adjective form or the noun form because a suffix is usually not emphasized orally.

Noun	Verb	Adjective
administra**tion**/administra**tor**	administra**te**	administra**tive**

Use a dictionary to fill in the following chart.

Noun	Verb	Adjective
science	X	scientific
	avail	available
	X	major
instruction		
	interact	
Some words do not have all three forms.		

EXERCISE 10 **Recognizing nouns used as adjectives**

If you looked up the words security *and* officer *in a dictionary, each would be listed as a noun. However, in the phrase* security officer, *while* officer *is acting as a noun,* security *is acting as an adjective. With a partner, fill in the blanks below with a noun from the box. Each noun will act as an adjective in the phrase.*

administration	chemistry	daycare
vocabulary	laser	sociology

1. _____ center

2. _____ instructor

3. _____ building

4. _____ book

5. _____ printer

6. _____ department

Can you think of other examples? Share those with the class.

One form of a verb is a participle.

- ► The present participle always ends in *-ing*.
- ► The past participle ends in *-ed* except for irregular verbs.
  - ► *walked* (regular verb)
  - ► *written* (irregular verb)
- ► Sometimes the participle is part of the verb phrase in a sentence.
  - ► *The students <u>are</u> **parking** in the parking lots right now.* (progressive tense)
  - ► *Those cars <u>are</u> **parked** by students.* (passive sentence)
- ► Sometimes the participle is used as an adjective.
  - ► *The tuition-<u>paying</u> students are angry.*
  - ► *The faculty parks in <u>reserved</u> spaces.*

EXERCISE 11   **Recognizing participles used as adjectives**

With a partner, choose the correct word in parentheses:

1. Other (frustrating, frustrated) students park their cars illegally in fire zones.

2. Students have become frustrated over the (limiting, limited) parking spaces

3. The (frustrating, frustrated) parking situation affects students academically.

4. The campus security officers ticket illegally (parking, parked) cars.

5. Students miss instructional time while driving around (crowding, crowded) parking lots.

Master Student Tip

Use a dictionary to make sure you are spelling a participle correctly. For example, *writing* has only one "t"; *written* has two. Also, *"I am hoping to solve the problem"* makes sense; *"I am hopping to solve the problem"* does not make much sense.

EXERCISE 12   **Deciding the difference in participial adjectives**

With a partner, decide when the present participle should be used as an adjective and when the past participle should be used as an adjective. Think of the difference between frustrated students *and* frustrating students.

Decide on how you would explain this difference to another student, and write your explanation here: _____

_____

_____

_____

_____

_____

_____

_____

_____

_____

EXERCISE 13 Reviewing a student's paragraph

Santo wrote a paragraph describing the parking problem at River Community College.

   A. *Read Santo's paragraph, and underline the word students each time it appears.*

   Student Sample 1

   Santo's Paragraph

   While there are several things that bother the many commuter students at River Community College, a major issue is the parking problem because the college does not have as many parking spaces as are required by these students. According to Officer Sandra Chartia, a college security officer, there are 8,250 students at the college but only 1,200 parking spaces. Therefore, even though 35 percent of current students take buses to the campus, there are still too few parking spaces for the students who drive to school. (personal communication, February 17, 2004) Because it is very difficult to find parking, many frustrated students have problems in their classes. My friend Maulik said that the students who arrive late to his Speech class usually miss a quiz and frequently are marked absent for the whole day, which affects their grade. Last fall, I had to quit my job since I had to get to campus early because of the parking situation. That was unfair. In my opinion, River Community College should find a way to fix this frustrating situation immediately.

   B. *For each instance, write down what Santo did, if anything, to make the noun more specific and interesting.*

   1. _____

   2. _____

   3. _____

   4. _____

   5. _____

   6. _____

   7. _____

▷ Writing, Editing, and Revising

EXERCISE 14 Writing your first draft

Reread Writing Assignment 1 (p. 169). Then use the information you have gathered, focused, and organized to write a first rough draft of your paragraph. Use the checklist to indicate what steps you have completed.

A. _____ Indent the first sentence of the paragraph.

B. _____ Leave margins on both the left and right sides of the page.

C. _____ Write a topic sentence.

D. _____ Write the major points and supporting ideas in complete sentences in the paragraph draft.

E. _____ Write a concluding sentence.

EXERCISE 15 Making your nouns more interesting

Reread your draft paragraph. Circle every noun. Write five of these nouns in the chart. Decide if you think the noun, by itself, is vague or interesting. Then write down any adjectives or adjective clauses from your paragraph that make these nouns more specific and interesting. If necessary, add adjectives or adjective clauses.

Noun	Rate your nouns 1 = very vague 5 = very interesting	Adjectives/Adjective clause
	1 2 3 4 5	
	1 2 3 4 5	
	1 2 3 4 5	
	1 2 3 4 5	
	1 2 3 4 5	

EXERCISE **16** Checking your writing

Reread your draft.

A. *Underline every verb. Circle every subject. How many clauses do you have? _____ How many subject-verb combinations? _____ How many sentences? _____*

B. *Check every verb to make sure you have the correct tense.*

C. *Run spell checker on your computer. Remember to be careful of overusing spell checker. You could be correctly spelling the wrong word!*

D. *Review your editing card.*

EXERCISE **17** Doing a peer response

Exchange your paragraph with another student. Using Peer Response Form 5-1 (p. 208), review the new paragraph.

SPOTLIGHT ON WRITING SKILLS

Word Processing

College students have to type their papers. Most credit-level instructors will not accept any handwritten assignments. If you are not comfortable typing your paragraphs, you should make improving your typing a priority.

You can sit down at a computer and copy paragraphs out of a book for practice. This will not only help your typing, it will increase your awareness of word endings, improve your spelling, and widen your vocabulary.

While you are practicing typing, take some time to check out all the features on the screen. Decide which fonts you like; notice how to justify margins, try out bullets and numbered lists; learn how to cut and paste; experiment with double-spacing. Use the Tools function to check your spelling and count the number of words in your paragraph.

POWER GRAMMAR

Sentence Variety

Good writers vary the length and types of sentences so that their writing is interesting to their readers.

Dependent clauses are frequently used in academic writing because they clarify not only the connection between clauses but also the relative importance of the two clauses. A writer should carefully choose which clause will remain independent and which clause will become dependent.

When a dependent clause begins a sentence, put a comma before the main clause.

A comma is not used when a dependent clause comes after the main clause.

Good writing contains **sentence variety.** Short sentences can add emphasis. Sentences with several clauses can help a reader understand the relationship between ideas because the dependent clauses begin with information words that clarify the relationships. However, too many long sentences can be boring and confusing for a reader.

Although several things bother students at River Community College, a major issue is *the* parking problem *because the college does not have as many parking spaces as are required by the students*

The most important clause states the topic of the paragraph, the parking problem. *The first dependent clause* is introductory and gives a general background for the topic. *The second dependent clause* gives the reason for the parking problem.

Last fall, I had to quit my job since I had to get to campus early because of the parking situation. That was unfair.

EXERCISE 18 Revising your paragraph

Reread your paragraph.

A. *Consider the comments made by your peer reviewer. Also, think of what you observed when you reviewed your partner's paragraph.*

▸ Do you clearly express your overall idea?

▸ Is your paragraph interesting and informative? Add more specific details if your information is too general.

▸ Are your nouns specific and powerful?

▸ How many sentences in your paragraph have more than one clause? _____ If you do not have sentence variety, combine some of your sentences, or break up some of your long sentences.

▸ Read your paragraph aloud to yourself. Does your writing have an interesting rhythm or is it choppy? If you do not like how your paragraph sounds, add some variety to your sentence structures.

B. *Rewrite your paragraph.*

C. *Submit your paragraph to your instructor. Be sure to attach the peer response form and your editing card to your paragraph.*

EXERCISE 19 Updating your editing card

When you receive your paragraph back from your instructor, make yourself a new editing card. At this point in the semester, you are beginning to prepare yourself for your writing after this class, so start with a fresh editing card. It is a new beginnig and you have made a lot of progress since this class began.

▸ *On one side of the new editing card, write the word* Success *and note all the errors from your old editing card that you no longer make.*

▸ *On the other side of the editing card, write the words* Needs Work *and note any errors that you made on this paragraph.*

EXERCISE 20   **Rewriting your paragraph**

Rewrite your paragraph, if necessary. Add your final paragraph and all drafts to your folder.

SPOTLIGHT ON WRITING SKILLS

Write for an Audience

Whenever you write, you write for your audience. Sometimes your audience will be only one reader, you, as when you make a grocery shopping list or freewrite. At other times, you do not know who the readers will be, as when you post a message in an Internet chat room or write a letter to the editor of a newspaper. Finally, there will be many times when you know very clearly who will be reading and responding to your writing, as when you are completing and exam or writing a letter to your college's President. Whenever you write, you adjust your writing to meet the needs and expectations of your reader(s).

EXERCISE 21   **Reading a student's paragraphs**

Read the following three paragraphs written by Santo, the student at River Community College. In small groups, discuss the differences you see in the three paragraphs. How did Santo adjust his vocabulary to the different audiences? What differences in sentence type and length do you notice?

Student Sample 2

Santo's E-mail to a Friend

> Hey what's up, do you know how bad to find a parking spot in school man???? It gets worse every time I get there yo . . . man my class starts at 9:30 and I gotta come to school like 1 or 2 hours early to find a good parking spot, cuz I don't wanna park far away from class . . . if I get there at like 9 or something I end up with parking at like all the way in the back and walk for another like 30 minutes or more . . . anyways, I'm out yo, peace.

Student Sample 3

Santo's Paragraph to the Student Newspaper

Dear Editor and Fellow Students,

The parking situation at River Community College is outrageous! There are a lot of students, but there are not enough parking spaces. We all know that you have to arrive on campus at least a half hour early just to find a parking space. Even then you frequently have to park far away from your classroom. Every morning, frustrated students speed around the parking lots, honking their horns and yelling at people. Students are missing classes and getting bad grades just because of the parking situation. It is time for us to do something about this problem, so all students who are sick and tired of hunting for parking spaces are invited to e-mail our college president, Dr. Lee Smith (lzsmith@rcc.edu), and demand increased parking spaces or free shuttle buses from off-campus parking lots.

Student Sample 4

Santo's Paragraph to the College President

Dear President Smith,

I would like to express my concern about the severe parking problem that students face at River Community College. There are several reasons why I am concerned about this problem. First of all, students miss essential instructional time as a result of having to drive around the crowded parking lots looking for a parking space. These tuition-paying students miss quizzes and tests and also do not know what is going on in class when they arrive late. As a result, they do poorly in their classes. Also, it is dangerous for evening students to have to go far away to park their cars and to walk long distances to their classes. Another reason I am concerned is that some students have become so frustrated over the limited parking that they have begun fighting over parking spaces. Other frustrated students park their cars illegally in fire zones, which would be catastrophic if an emergency occurred. If you do not realize how difficult the situation is for the students, you should, for one week, cancel all reserved parking spaces that are for college staff and have all the staff try to find parking. I think you should try to resolve this major problem by building a parking garage or by providing free shuttle buses from distant lots.

POWER GRAMMAR

Level of Formality

Writers choose to join clauses differently for different audiences.

Informal writing to a friend often contains few formal connectors. The reader probably knows a lot about the topic and does not need more clarity.

See you on Fri, I swear. I'll leave home real early.

The writer did not need to explain connection between *"See you on Fri"* and *"I'll leave home real early."*

Most **FANBOYS** are conversational and relatively informal, but they do clarify the relationship between independent clauses. (Review p. 69 for an explanation of FANBOYS and how to punctuate them.)

There are a lot of students, *but* there are not enough parking spaces.

FANBOYS emphasize **parallel** structure. (There is an independent clause on each side of the FANBOY.) Conversational English frequently uses parallel structure.

Transition words and expressions clarify the relationship between independent clauses. However, they are less conversational and more formal than FANBOYS. (Review p. 76 for an explanation of transition words and expressions and how to punctuate them.)

. . . when they arrive late. *As a result,* they do poorly in their classes.

What FANBOY would indicate the same relationship between these clauses? (Student Sample 4)

EXERCISE 22 Recognizing levels of formality

Combine the following independent clauses by using the connector in parentheses. Circle the audience(s) that would best fit this level of formality.

1. River Community College should open more parking lots for students. The students will not be late for class.   (so)

    _____

    _____

    Most appropriate audience(s)

    Friend / Fellow Students / College Administrator

2. Sanyi Thera has to park her car far away from the classroom building. She is always late for her class.   (therefore)

    _____

    _____

    Most appropriate audience(s)

    Friend / Fellow Students / College Administrator

3. We would like to meet on Wednesday at 3:00 p.m. We could arrange another time if 3:00 p.m. is not available. (However)

    _____

    _____

    Most appropriate audience(s)

    Friend / Fellow Students / College Administrator

4. You can speak with the director at the meeting. You can e-mail if you cannot attend.   (or)

    _____

    _____

    Most appropriate audience(s)

    Friend / Fellow Students / College Administrator

EXERCISE 23 **Evaluating levels of formality**

In groups of three, review your own freewriting, the example of personal e-mail (p. 178), and Santo's two paragraphs (p. 179). Each student should fill in her or his own chart with help from the other members of the group.

Audience	Examples of vocabulary appropriate to audience	Number of sentences with more than one clause	Examples of connectors	Rate the writing 1 = very informal 5 = very formal
Yourself (Freewriting)				
Friend (E-mail, Student Sample 2)				
College Students (Student Sample 3)				
College Administrator (Student Sample 4)				

► *Do the other members of your group agree with your evaluations? If not, discuss why you made different decisions.*
► *With the members of your group, answer this question: How did Santo adjust his writing to meet the needs and expectations of the different readers?*

Writing Assignment 2

Write a paragraph that seeks help from students at your college to solve the problem you are concerned about. This should be a persuasive paragraph. The audience for this paragraph will be the students at the college, whom you will address through a letter to the editor of your student newspaper.

▽ Gathering Information

You have already gathered information because this is the same topic you used in Writing Assignment 1. If you need more information, repeat some of the gathering processes that you developed in your action plan (p. 167).

▽ Focusing and Organizing

EXERCISE 24 Focusing your ideas

While you might not organize your thoughts if you were writing an e-mail to a close friend, you do not know which students will read your paragraph in the student newspaper, and you will not have a chance to explain what you meant if they do not understand your writing. Decide what one main idea about your issue you want to express to your fellow students.

EXERCISE 25 Developing a graphic organizer

Use a graphic organizer to focus your major points and supporting details. Choose whichever type of organizer you are comfortable with. Remember, it is your ideas you are organizing and your ideas you are going to express. Use the tools that you feel fit your needs and personality best.

SPOTLIGHT ON WRITING SKILLS

Using Introductions to Interest Your Audience

Because the students who read the student newspaper will not be required to read your paragraph, you must make it interesting and appealing. One way to increase the interest in your paragraph is to have an introduction that catches the attention of the reader.

Some Types of Introductions for a Paragraph:
- ► Dramatic statement
- ► Interesting fact or statistic
- ► Question
- ► Joke
- ► Polite, formal language
- ► Presentation of general issue
- ► Contrasting point of view

EXERCISE 26 **Analyzing the function of an introduction**

Read the following introductory sentences. Determine which introductory function each sentence serves.

1. Since there are 8,861 students at our college and only 1,100 parking spaces, there is an obvious problem. _____

2. Parking is a major problem for many businesses in our area.

   _____

3. The parking situation at River Community College is outrageous!

   _____

4. I would like to express my concern to you about the parking situation at River Community College. _____

EXERCISE 27 Rereading a student's paragraph

Look at Santo's paragraph to the student newspaper (Student Sample 3, p. 179).

    A. *Underline the introductory sentence. Why would this sentence attract the attention of students?*

    B. *Look at the second sentence of this paragraph. This is the topic sentence. Because the topic (parking situation) was introduced in the first sentence, the writer did not need to repeat those words, but the writer did explain his overall idea about the parking situation. Underline the writer's controlling, overall idea for this paragraph.*

    C. *You can add introductions to any paragraph. Look at Santo's first paragraph (Student Sample 1, p. 173). Underline the introduction. Notice that this introduction is only a clause, not a complete sentence. The information after this introductory clause gives the controlling idea, so this sentence is both the introduction and the topic sentence.*

EXERCISE 28 Adding an introduction

Review your graphic organizer. Determine what type of introduction you wish to have on this paragraph. Remember, this paragraph should appeal to students at your college.

Add an introduction to your graphic organizer.

SPOTLIGHT ON WRITING SKILLS

Reviewing the Functions of a Concluding Sentence

Concluding sentences can have a variety of functions. Concluding sentences can

- ► Restate the main idea
- ► Ask for a response
- ► Evaluate the topic
- ► Make a suggestion
- ► State a prediction

EXERCISE 29   Analyzing the function of a concluding sentence

Read the following concluding sentences. Determine which function each sentence serves.

1. The college should open more student parking lots, so students will not be late for classes. _____

2. If disciplinary action is taken against the drivers of illegally parked cars, people will think twice before they park on campus without a permit. _____

3. I think a solution to this terrible problem must be found as soon as possible. _____

EXERCISE 30   Evaluating concluding sentences

Review Santo's paragraph to the student newspaper (Student Sample 3, p. 179).

A. *Underline the concluding sentence. Is this sentence clear? Would students respond to it?*

B. *Review Santo's paragraph to the college president (Student Sample 4, p. 179). Underline the concluding sentence. Do you think the college president would be influenced by it?*

C. *Review Santo's first paragraph for his classroom instructor (Student Sample 1, p. 173). Underline the concluding sentence. Rewrite this concluding sentence to make it more direct and powerful.*

_____

_____

EXERCISE 31   Adding a concluding sentence

Review your graphic organizer. Determine what type of concluding sentence you wish to have on this paragraph. Remember, this paragraph should appeal to students at your college.

Add a concluding sentence to your graphic organizer.

▽ Writing, Editing, and Revising

EXERCISE 32 **Writing your first draft**

Write your paragraph to your student newspaper. Remember that your audience will be students at your college, so try to use vocabulary and ideas that would appeal to them.

EXERCISE 33 **Rereading your draft**

Reread your draft paragraph, and follow these steps to carefully edit your work:

A. Underline every verb. Circle every subject. Make sure that every clause has a subject and a verb.

B. Check that you have used the correct tense of every verb. If you chose to use passive voice, be sure you have constructed it correctly.

C. Check that you have an introduction that would attract students reading the college newspaper.

D. Check that you have a topic sentence with a clearly expressed controlling idea.

E. Check that you have sentences with major points and specific details that would appeal to students.

F. Check that you have a concluding sentence that clearly expresses what response you would like from students.

G. Make sure you have used vocabulary and sentence variety that would interest students.

H. Add adjectives or adjective clauses if your nouns are vague.

I. Run spell checker on your computer. If you are still not sure of the correct spelling of a word, use a dictionary.

J. Check your editing card to make sure that you are not making the same errors that you made in previous paragraphs.

EXERCISE 34 **Doing a peer response**

Exchange your paragraph with another student. Using Peer Response Form 5-2 (p. 210), review the new paragraph.

EXERCISE 35 Revising your writing

Reread your paragraph.

   A. Would students be eager to read it? If not, how can you make it more appealing? Read your paragraph aloud to yourself. Does it sound persuasive? Read your paragraph to a friend and ask for an evaluation. Strengthen your paragraph.

   B. Consider the comments your peer reviewer made. Also, think of what you observed when you reviewed your partner's paragraph. Did you notice any vocabulary that interested you? What did you find effective in that paragraph?

   C. Did you make errors in grammar or punctuation?

   D. Rewrite your paragraph.

   E. When you submit your paragraph to your instructor, attach your editing card and the peer response form.

EXERCISE 36 Updating your editing card

When you receive your paragraph back from your instructor, add to your editing card if you made any new types of errors. If you did not make an error that is already listed on your editing card, cross out that error and add it to the "Success" side of the card.

EXERCISE 37 Rewriting your paragraph

Rewrite your paragraph, if necessary. Place your revised paragraph and your drafts in your folder.

Writing Assignment 3

Write a paragraph that solicits help from the top administrator at your college or campus, whom you will contact through a letter. This should be a persuasive paragraph. The audience for this paragraph will be the administrator.

▷ Gathering Information

You have already gathered information because this is the same topic you used in Writing Assignments 1 and 2. If you need more information, repeat some of the gathering processes that you developed in your action plan (p. 167).

▷ Focusing and Organizing

EXERCISE 38 Constructing a graphic organizer

Choose the type of graphic organizer you would like to use for this paragraph. Remember, your decision depends on both the type of information you are expressing and your own preference for an organizational style.

   A. *Decide on the overall idea you wish to express to the college administrator.*

   B. *Think of what would be the most effective way to support that idea. Should the major points you wish to make be different from those you made in your paragraph to the student newspaper, or should some of them be the same? Should the supporting details be the same or different?*

   C. *Construct a graphic organizer to organize your ideas.*

EXERCISE 39 Adapting an introduction to your audience

Because you probably have a different relationship with the chief administrator of your college than you have with your fellow students, this paragraph will be different, more formal and less conversational. Your introduction should reflect that difference.

Some possible formal expressions to begin this paragraph are listed here:

▶ *I would like to express my concern about . . .*
▶ *As a student at (name of your college), I am interested in . . .*
▶ *To continue the high quality of education at (name of your college), (the situation) must be addressed.*

A. *Review Santo's paragraph to his college's president (Student Sample 4, p. 179), and underline the introduction.*
B. *Write a formal introduction to your paragraph on the top of your graphic organizer.*

▷ Writing, Editing, and Revising

SPOTLIGHT ON WRITING SKILLS

Making Verbs More Specific and Powerful

Just as nouns can be vague or specific, verbs also can be vague or specific. For example, the sentence *After the meeting, he went to his car* does not give a reader much information. The sentence *After the meeting, he went angrily to his car* gives the reader a better picture of how the man went to his car.

Adverbs are words like *slowly* and *fast* when they add information about "when", "where", "why", "how", and "how often" to sentences.

▶ Many adverbs end in *-ly* (e.g., *slowly, carefully, recently, quickly, immediately*).
▶ Some adverbs do not end in *-ly* (e.g., *late, fast, very, well, often*).

Adding *frequently* to the following sentence makes the sentence more specific and accurate, so the second sentence is clearer and more accurate.

1. *At River Community College, students have to park far away from their classrooms.*
2. *At River Community College, students frequently have to park far away from their classrooms.*

EXERCISE 40 Recognizing adverbs

In groups of three, locate and evaluate the use of adverbs in Santo's paragraphs.

  A. *One student locates an adverb in Santo's paragraph for the student newspaper (Student Sample 3).*
  B. *Another student decides why the writer added the adverb.*
  C. *A third student evaluates if the adverb made the sentence more effective.*
  D. *Switch roles and do the same activity for Santo's paragraph to his college's president (Student Sample 4). This paragraph has two adverbs.*

EXERCISE 41 Making verbs more interesting and more specific

Reread your draft paragraph.

  A. *Circle every verb.*
  B. *Write five of these verbs in the chart. Then write down any adverbs you have added to describe each verb, and state why you added the adverb.*

Verb	Adverb	Purpose of adding adverb

Remember, if you are not sure how to spell the adverb form of a word, use your dictionary.

EXERCISE 42 Adding adverbs

Add an adverb to any verb that <u>you think</u> needs to be more specific or more interesting.

EXERCISE 43 Hearing "Whaddya Say?"

In the first four chapters of this book, each Whaddya Say activity focused on a type of word ending that causes problems for ear learners of English. This final Whaddya Say contains examples of the various word endings: verb tenses, have/has, been/being, *and word forms. Listen carefully to your instructor, and fill in the blanks below. If you have difficulty hearing the word endings (and it is difficult!), think about what you have learned in this book to help you decide what the ending should be. Rely on both your oral skills and your knowledge of the English language.*

What we hear is not always what we write!

Fill in the blanks as you listen to this dictation.

1. The students _____ to _____ about the
    cafeteria because it _____ any pizza or tacos. They
    _____ copies of their _____ letters to the
    Student Senate, which _____ about the cafeteria
    since the beginning of last year. The students _____ that their
    _____ will _____ the Student Senate
    improve the cafeteria.

2. Budget cuts _____ the library. Last year, the library
    _____ open until 9:30 p.m. every evening. Before that, it
    _____ until 10 p.m. _____ . However, this
    year, the library _____ each evening at 9:00 p.m.

This means that students who _____ class until 9:30 p.m.

_____ to the library before it _____. When

the library _____ early, these students

_____ out books or _____ materials that

_____ on hold. Because the teachers still _____

the students _____ materials, these students _____

punished unfairly.

3. _____ to the _____ center? The center

_____ a student only one visit per week. In addition, a

_____ is _____ _____ only 15 minutes with

a student. _____ do not _____ enough time

to tutor students _____.

4. While many students _____ about their right

_____ other students have _____ _____

opinions about their right to clean air. The college _____ a

program _____ smoking to a few areas on campus. While

smoking _____, some non-_____ think

that this _____ enough. They want _____

measures that _____ smoking in all areas.

EXERCISE 44 Writing your first draft

*Write your paragraph to your college's administrator. Remember your
relationship to this administrator, who is your main audience, so try to use
vocabulary and ideas that would appeal to her or him.*

EXERCISE 45 Rereading your draft

Reread your draft paragraph, and follow this list to be sure you are carefully editing.

- **A.** Underline every verb. Circle every subject. Make sure that every clause has a subject and a verb.
- **B.** Check that you have used the correct tense of every verb. If you chose to use passive voice, be sure you have constructed it correctly.
- **C.** Check that you have an introduction that is appropriate for your reader.
- **D.** Check that you have a topic sentence with a clearly expressed controlling idea.
- **E.** Check that you have sentences with major points and specific details that would influence the college administrator.
- **F.** Check that you have a concluding sentence that clearly expresses what response you would like from the administrator.
- **G.** Make sure you have used vocabulary and sentence variety that would interest this reader.
- **H.** Add adjectives, adjective clauses, and adverbs if your thoughts are not clearly and accurately expressed.
- **I.** Run spell checker on your computer. If you are still not sure of the correct spelling of a word, use a dictionary.
- **J.** Check your editing card to make sure that you are not making the same errors that you made in previous paragraphs.

EXERCISE 46 Doing a peer response

Exchange both your paragraph to the student newspaper and the paragraph to the college administrator with another student. Do not exchange your paragraph with the student who already reviewed the newspaper paragraph. Using Peer Response Form 5-3 (p. 212), review both paragraphs.

EXERCISE 47 Revising your writing

Reread your paragraph. Follow these guidelines to improve your paragraph.

   A. Would a college administrator be persuaded by it? If not, how can you make it more persuasive?
   B. Consider the comments made by your peer reviewer. Also, think of what you observed when you reviewed your partner's paragraph. Did you notice any vocabulary that interested you? What did you find effective in that paragraph?
   C. Did you make errors in grammar or punctuation?

Rewrite your paragraph. When you submit your paragraph to your instructor, attach your editing card and the peer response form.

EXERCISE 48 Updating your editing card

When you receive your paragraph back from your instructor, add to your editing card if you made any new types of errors. If you did not make an error that is already listed on your editing card, cross out that error, and add it to the "Success" side of the card. Alternatively, since this is your last paragraph for this book, you might want to review all your editing cards and paragraphs from your folder to decide which specific features of writing or grammar will be your focus as you write independently in the future.

Remember—the course is almost over, but your growth and development as a writer is still ongoing. Build on your successes and commit to being the clearest, most interesting and most persuasive writer you can be.

EXERCISE 49 Rewriting your paragraph

Rewrite your paragraph, if necessary. Place your revised paragraph, all your drafts, and your interview notes in your folder.

▷ Additional Topics for More Practice and Assessment

Additional Writing Assignments

Since you have chosen this topic because you are truly interested in improving a situation at your college, you can actually send the paragraphs to your college newspaper and administrator. In addition, you could also write additional letters or articles if there are other people (e.g., alumni, city officials, members of campus organizations) you want to involve in the improvement of your campus situation.

Chapter 5 Self-Assessment

Answer the following questions on a separate sheet of paper, and put the sheet into your folder.

A. Go back to page 163, and check if you have accomplished the chapter's objectives. List the objectives you think you have accomplished in one column under the heading "Success." List the objectives you still need to practice in another column under the heading "Practice."

B. Answer these questions about the writing of an academic paragraph:

1. For a paragraph of 125 words, an introduction should not be longer than one sentence. Why would a longer introduction not be appropriate for a paragraph of this length?
2. A topic sentence must contain a controlling idea. What is a controlling idea?
3. Which part of a paragraph should be the longest? Why?
4. What are some purposes for a concluding sentence?
5. What is your overall opinion of graphic organizers? Discuss the pros and cons of using specific graphic organizers.
6. Why is it important to know the audience for your writing?
7. When you are self-editing your writing, what is most difficult for you?
8. What are some of the major differences between oral conversational English and written academic English?

9. At the beginning of the semester, what part of the writing process was most difficult for you—Gathering Information; Focusing and Organizing; or Writing, Editing, and Revising?

> ► In what ways do you think you have improved in this area?
> ► What difficulties do you still have in this area?
> ► How do you plan to improve your skills?

C. List three things that you will do in the next week to continue your improvement in writing.

D. List five ways that your writing skills have improved this semester.

WEB POWER

You will find additional exercises related to the content in this chapter at **http://esl.college.hmco.com/students**.

Appendix 1

▷ Transition Words

The charts below show some transition words and expressions and their "signal" to the reader.

Additional info	Contrasting info	Cause/Result info
also in addition furthermore moreover in fact	however on the other hand	therefore consequently as a result

An example	Time	A comparison	A list
for example to illustrate for instance	first at first next after that eventually at last	similarly in the same way	first first of all second finally most important

Appendix 2

Fanboys

An easy way to remember all the coordinating conjunctions is by remembering the term FANBOYS:

F or
A nd
N or
B ut
O r
Y et
S o

FANBOYS join grammar units of equal strength: [noun + noun], [verb + verb], [adjective + adjective], [sentence + sentence] . . .

Examples:

My <u>brother</u> or <u>sister</u> will help me finish my work. [noun + noun]
Her middle brother <u>is</u> very competitive and <u>wants</u> to win the game. [verb + verb]
The children are <u>busy</u> but <u>happy</u>. [adjective + adjective]
<u>Youngest children are usually very friendly</u>, so <u>they frequently seek careers that involve working with people</u>. [Independent clause, + independent clause]

When you join two sentences, you must put a comma in front of the FANBOY. The comma is a signal to your reader that another full sentence (subject-verb) is coming. If there is no comma, the reader will not expect another sentence (independent clause), and the reader could be confused.

Usually, coordinating conjunctions (cc) do not begin sentences in academic writing. Instead, they are used to join two independent clauses (ic).

Example: (1) Middle children in a family often have to compromise with their older and younger siblings, <u>so</u> (2) they often have easy-going personalities. [IC, cc ic.]

Appendix 3

PEER RESPONSE FORMS

Peer Response Form 2-1

Name of Writer: _____

Name of Reader: _____ Date: _____

Wide-Angle View   Format

Is the paragraph indented?   Yes   No

Is there only one indentation?   Yes   No

Does the writing go from margin to margin?   Yes   No

Organization

Is there a topic sentence?   Yes   No

Write the topic sentence here: _____

_____

How many major points support the topic sentence? _____

What are they? _____

Are there supporting details that describe the major points?   Yes   No

Give an example: _____

Close-Up View   Content

Put an * in the margin of the paragraph next to the information you found most interesting.

Zoom In

List any objectives: _____

List any adjective clauses: _____

List any verbs that confuse you: _____

▷ **Peer Response Form 2-2**

Names of Writers: _____

Names of Readers: _____ Date: _____

Wide-Angle View   Format

Is the paragraph indented?   Yes   No

Is there only one indentation?   Yes   No

Does the writing go from margin to margin?   Yes   No

Organization

Is there a topic sentence?   Yes   No

Write the topic sentence here: _____

_____

How many major points support the topic sentence? _____

What are they? _____

Did you understand the connections between the ideas in the sentences?
Yes   No   Sometimes

What did the writers do to help you understand the organization of the ideas?

_____

_____

Close-Up View   Content

What is the most interesting information in the paragraph? _____

_____

Zoom In

Give examples of the verb tenses used in the paragraph: _____

List any FANBOYS: _____

Are they punctuated correctly?   Yes   No

List any transition words or expressions: _____

Are they punctuated correctly?   Yes   No

▽ **Peer Response Form 3-1**

Name of Writer: _____

Name of Reader: _____ Date: _____

Wide-Angle View   Format

Is the format correct?   Yes   No

Organization

Is there a topic sentence?   Yes   No

Write the topic sentence here: _____

_____

How many major points did the writer use to support the topic sentence?

_____

What words did the writer use to show the logical connection between the

major points? _____

Close-Up View   Content

What is the most interesting information in the paragraph? _____

_____

Is this information the main idea, a major point, or a specific detail?

_____

Is the source of the information identified?   Yes   No

Zoom In

List any vocabulary words that the writer should define or explain: _____

_____

Does each sentence have a subject, a verb, and a period?   Yes   No

Are they any problems with verbs?   Yes   No

If yes, list the problem verbs: _____

Comments:

◹ Peer Response Form 3-2

Name of Writer: _____

Name of Reader: _____ Date: _____

Wide-Angle View   Organization

Does the topic sentence clearly identify the person and the occupation?
                         Yes   No

What is the writer's overall opinion about how well the person and the

occupation match? _____

What is one major point that the writer gives to support this opinion?

_____

How does the writer explain, clarify, or describe this major point?

_____

Close-Up View   Content

What is the most interesting information in the paragraph? _____

_____

Is this information the main idea, a major point, or a specific detail?

_____

Zoom In

Does the writer use any present perfect verbs?   Yes   No

If yes, write the subjects and verbs here: _____

_____

Does the writer use quotes?   Yes   No
If yes, are they punctuated correctly?   Yes   No
Does the writer use any reported speech?   Yes   No
If yes, is it used correctly?   Yes   No

Comments:

▷ **Peer Response Form 4-1**

Name of Writer: _____

Name of Reader: _____ Date: _____

Fill in this graphic organizer with information from the paragraph:

OPINION

↖ ↗

General Reason #1	General Reason #2

↕ ↕

Supporting Fact/Statistic	Supporting Fact/Statistic
Source:	Source:
Supporting Fact/Statistic	Supporting Fact/Statistic
Source:	Source:

↘ ↙

Conclusion

Did the writer give several reasons for her or his opinion?   Yes   No

Did the writer support each reason with a fact or statistic?   Yes   No

Did the writer cite the source for each fact or statistic?   Yes   No

Editing Help

How many different tenses does the writer use? _____

List one subject-verb combination for each tense that the writer used:

_____

_____

Does the writer use any passive voice verbs?   Yes   No

If yes, list the subject-verb combinations for any passive voice verbs in the

paragraph: _____

_____

Does the writer use any adjective clauses?   Yes   No

If yes, write one of the adjective clauses: _____

_____

List any transition words the writer used to help readers recognize when
he or she was moving from one major point to the next major point:

_____

Write down any sentence that you did not fully understand: _____

_____

_____

_____

▷ Peer Response Form 4-2

Name of Writer: _____

Name of Reader: _____ Date: _____

Organization

Does the topic sentence clearly state the writer's opinion?   Yes   No

What is the writer's opinion on smoking in public places? _____

_____

Fill in the graphic organizer with information from the paragraph.

BACKGROUND

Who was present? _____

Where did this occur? _____

When did this occur? _____

What adjectives describe the feelings of people during this event?

What happened first?

Then what happened?

Next?

Are the verbs in the correct tense? Do all the verbs have subjects?

Next?

What was the end of the incident?

How did this incident affect the writer's thinking about smoking?

If it was easy for you to fill in the graphic organizer, the story was probably clearly written in time order. If you had difficulty filling in the organizer, then the writer probably did not organize the paragraph clearly.

Did the writer tell the story in chronological (time) order?   Yes   No

Editing Help

How many different tenses does the writer use? _____

List one subject-verb combination for each tense that the writer used:

_____

_____

_____

Does the writer use any adjective clauses?   Yes   No

If yes, write one of the adjective clauses : _____

_____

List any transition words the writer used to help the readers understand

the sequence of events: _____

_____

Write down any sentence that you did not fully understand: _____

_____

_____

Did the writer list any errors that he or she was particularly looking for while editing the paragraph?   Yes   No

Write down any of these errors that the writer did not find and correct:

_____

_____

_____

▷ Peer Response Form 5-1

Name of Writer: _____

Name of Reader: _____ Date: _____

Organization

Does the topic sentence clearly state the writer's opinion, idea, or feeling about this issue?   Yes   No

What is the issue? _____

What is the writer's overall opinion, idea, or feeling about the issue?

_____

How does the writer support, explain, describe, or clarify this topic sentence?

_____

Does the writer have a concluding sentence?   Yes   No

In your opinion, what does this concluding sentence do for the paragraph?

_____

_____

_____

Content

What is the most interesting information in the paragraph? _____

_____

_____

Did you learn anything from this paragraph?   Yes   No

If yes, what did you learn? _____

_____

Write down any sentence that you did not fully understand: _____

_____

_____

_____

Editing Help

How many sentences are in the paragraph? _____

How many clauses are in the paragraph? _____

List two subject-verb combinations:

1. _____

2. _____

List any errors in subject-verb combinations or verb tenses:

Write down any adjective clauses in the paragraph:

Write down some adjectives from the paragraph:

Comments:

◸ Peer Response Form 5-2

Name of Writer: _____

Name of Reader: _____ Date: _____

Organization

What makes the opening attractive to the students reading the newspaper?

_____

What is the controlling idea in the paragraph? _____

_____

How did the writer support, explain, clarify, or describe the problem to the

students? _____

_____

What does the concluding sentence ask the students to do? _____

_____

Content

Which sentence did you like the best? _____

_____

Write down any sentence that you did not fully understand: _____

_____

Editing Help

What did the writer say he or she was carefully looking for during

self-editing? _____

List an example of where he or she was successful:

The student looked for _____. The student was

successful when he or she wrote _____.

List an example of where he or she was not successful:

The student looked for _____. The student was not

successful when he or she wrote _____.

How many sentences are in the paragraph? _____

How many clauses are in the paragraph? _____

List two subject-verb combinations:

   1. _____

   2. _____

Write down any adjective clauses in the paragraph:

Write down some adjectives from the paragraph:

Comments:

◁ Peer Response Form 5-3

Name of Reviewer: _____

Name of Writer: _____

Paragraph to Student Newspaper and Paragraph to the Highest Administrator of the College

Content and Organization

1. Each paragraph should have an interesting opening that would attract the attention of the intended reader(s). Does each paragraph have such an opening?   Yes   No

   a. What makes the opening attractive to the students reading the

   newspaper? _____

   _____

   b. What makes the opening attractive to the administrator reading

   the letter? _____

   _____

   c. What did the writer do differently in the two openings?

   _____

   _____

   d. Do you think the writer made appropriate distinctions in the two openings?   Yes   No

   Explain your answer. _____

   _____

   _____

2. Each paragraph should have a topic sentence that states the problem and the idea the writer will discuss about the problem. Does each paragraph have such a topic sentence?   Yes   No
   a. What is the controlling idea in the paragraph to the newspaper?

   _____

   b. What is the controlling idea in the paragraph to the

   administrator? _____

   c. Are the ideas the same?   Yes   No
   Why do you think the writer made them the same or different?

   _____

   _____

3. Each paragraph should have supporting information that supports, explains, clarifies, or describes the problem. Does each paragraph have such supporting information?   Yes   No
   a. How did the writer support, explain, clarify, or describe the problem to the students reading the newspaper?

   _____

   b. How did the writer support, explain, clarify, or describe the

   problem to the administrator? _____

   _____

   c. List some of the differences in how the writer developed the ideas in the paragraphs:

   Content: _____

   _____

   Vocabulary: _____

   _____

   Grammar: _____

   _____

   Relationship to reader: _____

   _____

4. Each paragraph should have a concluding sentence that calls for some sort of action. Does each paragraph have such a concluding sentence?   Yes   No

   a. What is called for in the newspaper paragraph?

   _____

   _____

   b. What is called for in the administrator's paragraph?

   _____

   _____

   c. Is the concluding sentence in each paragraph appropriate?
      Yes   No

   d. How does the writer make each concluding sentence appropriate for the intended reader(s)?

   _____

   _____

   Response requested: _____

   _____

   _____

   Vocabulary: _____

   _____

   _____

   Grammar: _____

   _____

   _____

   Relationship with reader: _____

   _____

   _____

Editing Help

1. What did the writer say he or she was carefully looking for while

   self-editing? _____

   List examples of where he or she was successful:

   The student looked for _____. The student

   was successful when he or she wrote _____.

   The student looked for _____. The student

   was successful when he or she wrote _____.

   List examples of where he or she was not successful:

   The student looked for _____. The student

   was not successful when he or she wrote _____.

   The student looked for _____. The student

   was not successful when he or she wrote _____.

2. How many sentences are in the paragraph to the student

   newspaper? _____

3. How many sentences have only one clause? _____

4. How many sentences are in the paragraph to the administrator?

   _____

5. How many sentences in this paragraph have more than one clause?

   _____

Index